Blank

Blank

Why it's fine to falter and fail, and how to pick yourself up again

GILES PALEY-PHILLIPS & JIM DALY

Hardie Grant

QUADRILLE

Publishing Director: Sarah Lavelle
Senior Commissioning Editor: Céline Hughes
Cover Designer: Jack Smyth
Head of Design: Claire Rochford
Typesetter: Seagull Design
Head of Production: Stephen Lang
Production Controller: Sinead Hering

Published in 2021 by Quadrille,
an imprint of Hardie Grant Publishing

Quadrille
52–54 Southwark Street
London
SE1 1UN
quadrille.com

Cataloguing in Publication Data: a catalogue record for this book is
available from the British Library.

Text © Giles Paley-Phillips and Jim Daly 2021
Design and layouts © Quadrille 2021

ISBN: 978 1 78713 616 8

Printed in China

JIM – For Miranda and Maria.

GILES – For Michelle, Elijah and Sonny, and every single one of our wonderful guests, who have given me more understanding of what it means to be human than I've ever experienced before in my life.

Contents

Overwhelmed

Speechless

Stuck

Fearful

Blocked

Alone

Stalled

Blank

Isolated

Thwarted

Stumped

Frustrated

Stifled

Empty

Distant

Going Blank:
An Introduction to
the *Blank Podcast*

Sometimes we think we need to totally believe in ourselves or we need to be totally perfect before we can take action, but actually it's the opposite: action actually gives us confidence to continue and to take any steps to make something better.

Dr Radha Modgil

In 2004, while I was going through a downward period in my creativity, feeling unfocused and despondent, I decided to write down all the things I wanted to achieve or do in the next ten years.

A bold move, you might think, but I reckoned it would give me a set of problems to solve, tests to pass, goals to score. Some were fairly doable, some were downright ludicrous (or so I believed at the time), many were forgettable, but one really stayed with me, even after I'd lost that piece of paper two or three years in!

The sorts of things I put on that piece of paper ranged from visiting New York (not done that yet) to having five books published (I have done that one); from learning the piano (nope, not yet) to running the London Marathon (tick! Did it in 2016, a bit behind schedule).

BLANK

But that one idea I always kept in the recesses of my own creative locker?

Making a podcast.

Why this particular idea continued to appeal to me when so many others evaporated remains a mystery, but for many years it was just a pipe dream. I'd never had any real broadcast experience or learned production skills, and furthermore, I had no clue what this podcast would be about.

Fast-forward to 2018. I was in a similar slump to the one I'd been in in 2004 – nothing was coming out of me creatively, my mojo was flaccid, and I was in need of some artistic Viagra to kick-start a new project. Could a podcast be just the thing to help?

It was the start of a golden age for podcasts, with some 550,000 in existence at the time, covering a huge number of topics and genres – the arts, politics, comedy, sports, fanzines, drama, music, kids' shows and so on. One kind of podcast that was fairly prevalent was the long-form interview, and this was the type of show that intrigued me the most: the chance to sit and shoot the shit with inspirational individuals was something that truly appealed to me.

But how do you approach that in a different way to everyone else? I thought about what I'd like to listen to, what would benefit me as a creative person, what would help me right now, but I found I couldn't think of anything: my mind was blank. And that's when it hit me.

Attempting to find those little universalities that are very human experiences is not always easy, but in precisely that moment of blankness – when I seemingly couldn't think of anything – I'd stumbled upon the very thing that would be perfect to investigate.

The blankness I was experiencing was not just about struggling to think of a podcast subject – it was the very thing I was battling in my creative life as a whole. If I was honest with myself, I'd been going blank for quite some time, and would be blank again many more times in the future – so what better subject to tackle?

But how do you set up a podcast? What are the mechanics? How does it work? I didn't think I could do this on my own, so I needed a co-pilot – someone to collaborate with. Collaboration has been something I've long enjoyed, going back to my days playing in bands. I find that team spirit incredibly energising.

Enter stage left: Jim Daly.

Jim and I knew each other through social media, having had a few interactions, and those who listen to the podcast will be very aware of our love of Crystal Palace FC, and that Jim hosts and produces FYP, a Crystal Palace fanzine podcast. As a listener, I'd always enjoyed Jim's relaxed, light-hearted delivery, and I knew he would be great for this project I was dreaming up.

The concept I had at that point was a long-form interview podcast with various well-known people, talking to them about those blank moments in their creative lives when things were not working quite so well. Initially, I thought we would just be talking to writers and actors, but when Jim and I sat down together in a café in Brighton one afternoon in July 2018, we started to see the potential for widening our scope.

Why stop with writers and actors? Sportspeople, comedians, business people, politicians – they'd definitely have blank moments too. Indeed, quite early on in our first meeting, it became obvious that Jim himself was having a blank period in his career. He'd got the fear of doing stand-up comedy, and as much as I felt for him in his situation, I was also pleased to find a like-minded person who would have the level of empathy we would need to allow our guests to feel comfortable enough to open up about their own blanks.

So, that afternoon we hatched a plan, we recorded a little promo video, and the *Blank Podcast* was born. Then I went home and threw together some artwork on Photoshop, and set about trying to find some guests!

I cast the net out far and wide, thinking that maybe one or two people might say yes. I even thought I'd try my luck with a few big names – after all, the worst that could happen was a no. But to my utter astonishment, my Twitter DMs starting filling up with yes after yes; people were totally getting the concept and looking forward to the idea of talking about it!

The very best thing about podcasts, and I think this is what attracts guests to the medium, is that you can really be yourself, and it's an opportunity to talk candidly without any big sells. And that's exactly what we wanted: an hour of unedited chat over a cup of tea, and for our listeners to feel like they were sitting at the next table, listening in.

We decided early on that, as a cottage-industry-style endeavour, we'd be doing everything ourselves – booking guests and venues, hosting, recording, producing, editing and marketing – and it might be wise to work with a podcast platform that could have our back when we needed it. So, we signed up with Acast, and set up our inaugural recording sessions.

Our first day of recording was at my house, with three guests from my local area spaced out over the course of the day: the screenwriter Warren Dudley, children's author Lindsay Galvin and *Game of Thrones* actor Daniel Tuite. It was always our intention to be a little bit different from the kind of long-form interview podcasts that often reminded us of the now infamous – and at times tense – one-to-one between Sir David Frost and President Richard Nixon. These work well, of course, but having a third voice felt like a nice dynamic for us and provided another perspective to the discussion. I was a little nervous at first, but within minutes I forgot we were being recorded. It felt just like I wanted it to feel – three people around a table with a cup of tea, chatting about life, careers and those difficult blank moments.

The thing that struck me then and continues to amaze me now – and it's why this podcast has continued to evolve as much as it has – is the sheer scope of what 'blank' can mean to different people. It isn't just about how we 'go blank' creatively; it's about when things are not going well in any given situation. It's a state of mind that comes out in different ways for each individual, whether that's public failure, social anxiety, grief or imposter syndrome. As we've continued along this journey, it has continued to be interpreted in so many new and different ways.

GOING BLANK

By September of that first year, when we sat down with the wonderful Jon Ronson in his hotel room in Soho one dreary Friday afternoon, I almost felt like I was having an out-of-body experience and that it must be someone else doing this – and that feeling has never quite gone away. Forget what the naysayers tell you – meeting your heroes is amazing, and long may it continue.

This podcast has genuinely been one of the greatest things I've ever been involved in, and it's a privilege to make. As labours of love go, this has been the very best.

JIM

I can't take any credit for this podcast – the idea was all Giles's – but when he pitched the outline to me over a cup of tea and a tiffin in a quiet café in Brighton, I knew it was something I wanted to be involved in. What I didn't know was just how much I would discover about life, work and myself in the next couple of years.

The idea itself was a pretty simple but solid one: talk to people who have been successful in a range of creative fields about those moments when things don't go quite so well. Maybe we'd learn a bit about how to get through those moments, maybe we'd hear some funny stories, maybe we'd get to feel a bit better about ourselves by hearing that famous people have the same issues we do.

What we got instead, over the 100 or so episodes since then, is so much more. Not only have I met some heroes of mine – all of whom have turned out to be absolutely, brilliantly lovely people, forming some incredible memories I'll never forget (and gaining me a few very famous Twitter followers along the way) – I have also made a lifelong friend in Giles. I knew of him through Twitter, of course, and also because we were (and still are, for our sins) Crystal Palace fans. But I knew the minute we started chatting on that sunny afternoon by the sea that we were destined to be mates forever. He is such a kind soul and he also shares the same hopes, fears, creative ambitions and worries about life that I do. I knew even then that if this podcast didn't end up being a success, it didn't matter, as I'd have at least made a really good friend out of it – and in a way, that was more important.

Making connections to other people is so vital, and it's what forms the crux of the *Blank Podcast*. It's certainly what keeps me going. There are episodes we do with people I'm a massive fan of, and other episodes we do with guests I don't know quite as much about, but I always come away feeling somehow enriched and full of happiness, and like I've just added a really interesting person to my life. That connection with Giles when we first met was really key, and the connections we make with our guests on the podcast not only lead to great conversations (that we hope our listeners enjoy too) but also some really useful nuggets of truth and life lessons. I always come away from an episode with a few, and I've tried to apply as many of them as possible to my life since – some successfully, some less so.

In fact, I was having a pretty big blank moment in my own creative life when Giles proposed the podcast: I had been doing comedy for five years and it hadn't quite gone the way I'd have liked. I'd grown frustrated by the lack of progress, which was nearly all my fault, and I needed something to jump-start my career. I secretly hoped that doing the podcast might help me learn a bit about why I had stalled, and maybe give me some pointers to getting back on track. What I didn't realise was that I would be getting one-on-one advice from some of the UK's most successful comedians, and that just over a year later, I would have performed at the Edinburgh Fringe and got myself a comedy agent.

So, I owe a lot to this podcast and to Giles. It's given me the chance to meet so many brilliant people – and not just in the creative fields. It started off that way, but very quickly we realised we could broaden our scope to include business people, scientists, politicians and many more. In fact, the only guest so far that I have got super nervous about meeting was Caroline Lucas, leader of the Green Party. I am a card-carrying member of the Green Party and I just think she's brilliant and such an inspiration. She's like a rock star to me, so to get to meet her was such a big deal. Thankfully, she was lovely, and she even gave us one of the best going-blank stories we've ever heard, which is included in this book.

I do hope that you get as much out of this book – our little journey through blankness and all the various aspects of going blank – as I have from the last two years of making our podcast. In it, we will explore the various themes of 'blankness': those moments when things just aren't going right; when you're staring at a blank document trying to be creative or express yourself; when you go blank on stage or halfway through a presentation; when you falter during a performance; or when you're having a monumental life blank in which everything is going wrong. We have hand-picked the best advice and anecdotes from our podcast guests and added our own thoughts and experiences on the areas of blankness that keep coming up on the podcast. You'll find us talking about everything from creativity to grief, lack of sleep to social media, social awareness to public failure. We hope you'll learn something interesting along the way, just as we have with the podcast.

Chapter 1:
Public Failure

I'm a firm believer in fault versus responsibility ... and I mean absolute and total responsibility for every single part of your life, every single one: your health, your wealth, your house, your kids, your mental health, your physical health, your friendships, your failures – definitely your failures, as well as your successes. Everything. If you can do that, it's the most empowering thing.

Jake Humphrey

'I have not failed,' Thomas A. Edison is said to have declared when talking about his relentless quest to create a light bulb. 'I've just found 10,000 ways that won't work.'

We've all experienced those moments when our stomach starts churning, our hands feel clammy, beads of sweat start to trickle gently down our face, every eye in the room is focused on us, and there's that overriding desire to flee as quickly as possible – whether it's running off a stage or just metaphorically retreating inside ourselves. Of all the subjects that come up on the podcast, the theme of public failure is one that crops up a lot. And when it came to writing about it for this chapter, the first thing that popped into my head was a moment in my childhood that now feels fairly innocuous, but at the time felt very real and very humiliating.

BLANK

I must have only been around seven or eight years old. I had been taken to our local Anglican church by my family and coerced into joining the Servers of the Sanctuary, which sounds a bit like the latest album by Megadeth but was in fact a selection of willing congregants who performed duties throughout the Sunday service.

There were several roles undertaken by the servers, including the Crucifer (surprisingly, not a character from WWE), the Acolytes (a 1960s backing group) and the Thurifer. My mission, being the youngest of this merry gang of worshippers, was that of the Boat Bearer. Like a reluctant hobbit venturing into the burning wasteland of Mordor with ring in hand, I had to guard this concaved receptacle at all times as I wandered about the sanctuary behind my commanding officer, the Thurifer. His purpose during the proceedings was to carry the thurible, a metal censer suspended from chains, in which incense was burned during the service. My boat carried the incense granules

that were sporadically scattered over the heated coals and
then used to bless just about anything going – the priest, the
scriptures, the communion wafers, the congregation ... whatever
the Thurifer could wave that thing at, he would.

I did not take lightly the responsibility of carrying out my
duties; even at a young age I knew that I couldn't let anyone
down. All eyes would be upon me, and I felt the weight of the
expectations of everyone in attendance. Maybe it was this, or
maybe it was the heavy cassock I had to wear, or the length of
time spent standing and the vomit-inducing incense, but in
that first service, my eyes started to go blurry, my legs started
to wobble and my head began to spin. I collapsed on to the floor
and was whisked away to the back of the building, where my
head was shoved between my knees to aid my recovery.

This last part may have seemed quick to those looking on, but
for me the events took place in slow motion, and having to pass
all those expectant faces on both sides as I was helped down
the aisle of the church was a fairly torturous walk of shame.
My public failure was complete.

But as I have looked at this subject more broadly since, through
doing the podcast, one thing stands out from what I now
understand about public failure: it is nearly always in our own
heads that we build these moments up, and we are the ones
who inflict the most punishment on ourselves.

It was when speaking to Crystal Palace chairman Steve Parish
that the idea of chastising ourselves while in the midst of failure
struck home. Steve spoke about how, if the team has lost, it can
soften the blow if you go out after the game, while if you win, it's
better to stay at home. Doing the 'opposite' of what's expected
can help in those moments, because in losing you are dealing
with a public failure.

Steve takes his responsibilities to the club extremely seriously, and it's a burden of responsibility that can be intense at times. For him, a real sackcloth-and-ashes moment is if he heads to Twitter after a defeat. It's a form of self-flagellation, a punishment to reinforce all the mistakes that he may have made. As Steve told us, so much is riding on what the football club is trying to do that it isn't just losing a game of football – it's so much more than that.

The roots of this kind of self-imposed punishment can be seen throughout history. In the Middle Ages, people would seek to cleanse themselves of diseases through public whippings – and this sentiment remains today, it's just that the method and equipment we use have evolved.

We often feel this need to respond to public failure by punishing ourselves publicly, because of overwhelming feelings of guilt. For Steve, it's the weight of responsibility he has taken on, and the expectations of the team, the people he employs and, of course, the fans. There are all these elements that he has to get right, and many people he has to please. That perception that we are letting others down by our actions is what makes public failure all the more painful.

BLANK

But sometimes this public humiliation is thrust upon us, and no one is more aware of this process than Jon Ronson – he's spoken at great length on the subject, and even wrote a book about it called *So You've Been Publicly Shamed*. Jon was one of our first guests on the *Blank Podcast*, and this was definitely an area Jim and I wanted to pursue with him.

Jon was stark when he spoke about his time making and researching the book, and about those times when one mistake can cause Twitter to destroy someone and leave them feeling humiliated and ashamed. There's also this idea that they are a victim of a kind of identity theft, because they are being judged for some tiny little sliver of their lives by people who don't actually know anything about them.

And Jon wasn't just talking about public figures, either – it's often regular people who aren't used to public exposure. He explained to us how public shaming is, in essence, an excommunication from a community: these people are being told that they aren't good enough, and in reading these things being said about them, they can start to believe them, and even feel depressed or contemplate suicide or self-harm.

JIM

Caroline Lucas is someone who knows all about being in the spotlight. As the Green Party's first-ever MP (and, at the time of writing, their only MP), she's currently ploughing a lonely furrow in Westminster – and being so visible means any slip-ups are likely to be jumped on, especially by opposition politicians. Thankfully for her, her worst moment in Parliament came early on in her career.

After the respectful and organised atmosphere of the European Parliament, where Caroline was an MEP before being elected to Westminster, the chaotic nature of the House of Commons couldn't have been more different. In Brussels, everyone sat in silence as they listened and waited for their turn to speak; in Westminster, MPs are constantly talking over each other, and Caroline very quickly realised she had to be comfortable standing up and interrupting people if she felt she had a strong counter-argument in order to get her opposition on the record.

A few weeks in, having interjected a few times, she was feeling confident. So, one afternoon during an education debate, she shot up to intervene again, shouting, 'Will the honourable member give way?!' – which they duly did, only for Caroline to stand there and suddenly realise she had no idea what she was going to say.

To fill the embarrassed silence, she started talking about nothing in particular while her brain whirred away trying to find the words, until she had to give up and admit she couldn't remember what she was going to say. Mortified, she sat down, hoping the ground would swallow her up – and then she remembered that Hansard, the official report of everything said in the House of Commons, would have recorded all of this. Checking the next day, she was relieved to learn they had just put three little dots instead of her saying she had forgotten what she was going to say. Whoever was in charge of Hansard had been kind to her that time!

What's great about Caroline's anecdote, and about Caroline in general, is her desire to learn from her mistakes. To this day, she always takes a notepad with her to Westminster, to jot down anything she wants to talk about. And what was refreshing about her story was her honesty and openness. Yes, she screwed up in a fairly public way at the highest level of politics in this country, but even then it was okay. It was like she was telling Giles and me that any mistake is salvageable and can provide a learning opportunity.

I like to think that when I make mistakes in the future – although hopefully not in the Houses of Parliament in front of 600 MPs – I, too, will add a (metaphorical) notepad to future endeavours. If we all approached our mistakes head-on like Caroline, maybe we wouldn't lose so much time beating ourselves up about them and worrying about what people thought of us. And her story shows us that even in the House of Commons, a frankly archaic system and building that prides itself on people tearing each other apart to score political points, there was a moment of kindness as Hansard – which is supposed to record every single word, 'um' and 'er' that MPs

BLANK

utter in the House (in theory to hold them accountable to the public, as it is us that votes them in there) – was kind to Caroline with those three little dots.

If there can be kindness in the Houses of Parliament, and if Caroline can be kind to herself after that mistake, then we can all be a bit kinder to ourselves when we make mistakes. That's certainly what I will try to do from now on.

ALICE IN WANDERLUST

In 2018, a new online forum called Tattle Life came into being – a place where people could go and commentate on those who monetise their personal lives online. It's an environment where criticism is actively encouraged. But its recent prominence in the press has come from accusations of harassment of high-profile YouTubers and bloggers, who have seen the site's proclaimed 'commentary' remit descend into bullying and trolling. The majority of users claim to be 'anti-fans', and use the forum to voice their disdain and vitriol for those whose popularity has flourished. That such a place exists to facilitate group hate is a sad indictment of where we are as a society.

The story of Clemmie Hooper, a prominent 'mummy blogger' and 'Insta-mum' shone a spotlight on the darker elements of this site. Clemmie had a huge online following of fellow mums, who appreciated the candid approach to motherhood displayed on her Instagram account, Mother of Daughters.

In early 2019, a Tattle Life user called Alice in Wanderlust started to raise suspicions among the mummy influencers. For some eight months, this account had been posting derogatory comments regarding various Insta-mums and bloggers, even going so far as to make racist remarks about some prominent black mums. Playing detectives, some users noticed that Alice's geo-tags often matched the locations of Clemmie's Instagram posts, and when other bloggers called her out, the weight of suspicion became too much for Clemmie and she issued an apology.

Despite her apology, the damage had very much been done, and within days she had lost more than 10,000 followers. Clemmie's true motivations have still not been fully explained, and her apology was greeted with a fair amount of scorn and cynicism by those affected and by the wider Insta-mum community. The subsequent pile-on derided her claims that she had started to post from the Alice in Wanderlust account as a way to infiltrate and influence users who had targeted her and her family, only to end up being drawn in to the trolling and consumed by it.

The fallout was swift and brutal. Clemmie deleted her Instagram account, her husband was seen to be very publicly distancing himself from her behaviour, and many people were calling for her to be struck off as a practising midwife – something Clemmie was doing part-time alongside her online work.

Writing on Instagram, the mummy blogger Laura Rutherford (aka That Mummy Smile) addressed 'Alice in Wanderlust': 'I don't owe it to you to remain quiet. You've goaded and encouraged trolls to tear my reputation apart for the last eight months. Mine and a handful of other influencers – and for what gain?'

And it is this last line – 'and for what gain?' – that will continue to provoke debate, as the stakes for tumbling down the rabbit hole of trolling others, if caught out, are extremely high.

Indeed, for Clemmie, the decision to delete the very thing she has made her name and money from – her Instagram account – must have been an extremely bitter pill to swallow, particularly as it wasn't her conduct on Instagram that lead to this moment.

BLANK

Clemmie ultimately suffered the severe consequences of her actions, in the end being both the 'shamer' and the 'shamed' in this instance. It's as if she suffered a blank moment in judgement that escalated and spiralled into a sustained period of extreme blankness – something we talked about on the podcast with Jon Ronson.

Jon told us that lots of social scientists say that violence is more awful when it's being committed for moral purposes. So if a person feels like they're killing somebody for moral reasons, that they've got morality on their side, the violence is often worse. And you can draw a parallel with what happens during a lot of social-media shaming – it's brutal because the people doing it are doing it in the name of morality. Of course, not all social-media shamings are the same – sometimes somebody has done something really bad and they need to be made an example of, but quite often it's just some stupid nothing thing that people are turning into something huge.

Failure in all its forms is an inevitable part of life, and once you realise this, you can start the process of developing a more positive attitude towards it – by seeing failure as an opportunity, a moment to take a step forward rather than back.

What doing the podcast has shown me, time and time again, is that even the most successful people have their own moments of public failure – and while those moments play a part in who they are, those failures do not define them. For me, the *Blank Podcast* has allowed me to own my failures by talking openly about them and reflecting on how they have pushed me on. I mean, the very fact that our podcast is unedited means that, most weeks, there are little mistakes on air that Jim and I might notice but listeners might not, and this goes back to that story of my younger self being dragged away from the sanctuary and the idea that failure is in the eye of the beholder. Most of the time, failure is what we see, and others don't.

JIM

Public failures always hit hard, no matter whether you are prepared for them or not. There are people like Justine Sacco, who was completely oblivious to her public failure as she was 35,000 feet up in the air. She had sent a tweet containing a really insensitive – and frankly terrible – joke about AIDS to her 170 followers before boarding a flight to South Africa. By the time she landed, eight hours later, her tweet had been retweeted a million times and she had been fired from her job.

Then there are people like me. Working as a stand-up comedian and a presenter, I'm asking for very public failures every time I step on stage or in front of a camera. My only saving grace is that the sort of gigs I perform at and the sort of shows I make have very few people watching. But then, Justine Sacco only had 170 followers, so she probably thought the same thing.

And it still really hurts when things go wrong. A couple of years ago, I was performing at a charity gig where Milton Jones was headlining. I had performed hundreds of gigs over the previous few years, so I was, in a way, very experienced, but it was my first time back doing stand-up after a year or so trying to make it as a TV presenter (more on that later).

The MC for the night, an excellent comedian called Bennett Arron, warmed up the crowd perfectly. Not too hot, not too cold – like the Goldilocks of MCing gigs, he had them simmering just right for the opening act.

First on was James Sherwood, a brilliant pianist-turned-comedian who takes a keyboard out on stage with him, doesn't use it for the first 15 minutes of his 20-minute set, and then blasts out some hilarious tunes on it, with the anticipation making the gags land even better.

Then it was me. I had done middle spots at countless gigs before, some of them alongside the likes of Reginald D. Hunter, Gary Delaney and Seann Walsh, so I knew my ten-minute set like the back of my hand, and this night it started out fine. But for some reason, about three or four minutes in, I could feel I was losing the room. It was like someone was turning down the thermostat, and the warmth of the gig slowly seeped out of me and the venue.

Doing stand-up well or badly is like having an out-of-body experience. You can see yourself on stage from the back of the room, and you can feel what the audience is feeling. When it's going well, it's incredible, but when it starts going badly, it's like watching a car crash – only you're the one driving the car, and there's no way to stop it happening.

Normally, if the first minute or so of a gig goes well, then you're away, but this time, despite a good start, it just wasn't working. With a short set, there's always a sense of just getting to the closing joke, which is normally one of your best gags, and getting off stage. But I didn't even get that far before one of the most chilling things that has ever happened to me on stage occurred.

Straight after the punchline for yet another joke that didn't land, there was a pause – and if that happens, you know it's not going well, because normally you only pause to allow for laughter. During this painful silence, as I was trying to draw all the strength I had left to launch into my next joke, I heard one of the youngish lads in the front row turn to his mate and whisper, 'He's dying.'

Whisper! That's how quiet it was – that I could hear him WHISPER to his friend. Bless him, he had tried to conceal his jab at me, but I still heard it.

It was one of those moments in which you can't pretend any more that anything other than a complete catastrophe is taking place. Up until that point, I could have got through to the end, got off stage and back into the comfort of the green room, and pretended to myself that it went 'okay', that maybe the audience was having an off-night (despite howling with laughter at all the other acts), and it was just about all right. But hearing 'he's dying' gave me no other option than to accept defeat.

Milton Jones was very complimentary after the gig, in that way that people are when they're trying to make you feel better, but I knew I'd publicly had a mare. It wasn't a huge audience – 150 max, maybe – but it was enough to leave me feeling devastated, enough to be a public failure. I had been there to make them laugh and I didn't.

BLANK

It was a hard drive home, after that gig. I honestly did think about packing it in. I'd been going for five or so years at this point, and many of my peers who had started at the same time as me were now playing club gigs, getting agents and TV shows, going on tours and generally doing amazingly. Meanwhile, I was dying in a school hall.

I should have been doing better at that stage and I clearly wasn't, but I knew, deep down, two things:

1) I still wanted to do stand-up. After every previous bad gig, I'd still gone back to it and tried again. There's something about stand-up that has made me incredibly persistent in my comedy career, and that determination has seeped into other things I do professionally too. I think the idea of giving up is so embarrassing, having told the world that this is what I do, that

I'd rather soldier on – even if it means being terrible. I knew I couldn't face my family, my friends and the world in general and say, 'I'm giving it up, I've failed.' And if I never give up, well, then I'll never fail, will I?

2) I knew, in my gut, that my performance that night was my fault. It wasn't the audience, it wasn't the MC, it wasn't the venue … it was me. I hadn't gigged much recently, I was rusty as hell and it showed in my performance. I needed to take some responsibility for my mistakes, and doing so would, in turn, give me the power to do something about them.

And I did. Okay, not until about two years later, but I still did it! I now have an agent, a new show, and I'm (hopefully) better at stand-up, with a new-found confidence in my material. I look forward to getting on stage now, and when things do go wrong, I try to just let it wash over me and see it as part of the process.

———

Not meeting other people's expectations is a hard pill to swallow and can leave you with regrets – something the former Manchester United star and current TV pundit Gary Neville opened up about with us, particularly regarding his ill-fated spell at Valencia. In December 2015, Neville was made manager of the Spanish first division side, having been assistant manager of the England national side before that. His first foray into full-time management didn't go well. Not being able to speak Spanish proficiently didn't help, something that was questioned by fans and journalists upon his appointment, while others wondered why he had left a successful career in broadcasting with Sky Sports, where he had been building a reputation as the best new pundit around after ending his trophy-laden 19-year career as a player.

It was a risk, and one that didn't start well, with his new side recording a sequence of nine winless games in La Liga. Having failed to improve the team's form, and after a seven-nil humiliation against Barcelona, Neville was sacked less than four months after his appointment. At the time of his departure, Valencia were 14th in the league, only six points clear of the relegation zone, and had won only three of 16 league games with him as manager, in which they also failed to keep a single clean sheet.

Gary told us that managing and coaching hadn't been something he really wanted to pursue once he hung his boots up, because he knew that, with coaching, you have to immerse yourself in it every second of every day. But then England manager Roy Hodgson had asked him to join the coaching team in 2012, and Gary felt like it fitted around his burgeoning broadcast career.

BLANK

Juggling those two roles was going fine until he was asked to take over at Valencia (which was owned by a friend of his) just until the end of the season. Gary told us he kicks himself to this day that he said yes, and for the 'stupid' mistakes he made there. These included not taking experienced staff with him (including any that spoke Spanish), not changing the squad to gain a bit of authority and control, and not showing strong enough leadership. All things he has been able to recognise as errors since, but not at the time. When it all came crashing down, he knew he was going to get criticised.

What's interesting about Gary's admissions here, apart from his honesty, is that there are so many of them. It's hard enough for us to admit when we've messed up once, but to reflect on numerous failings takes real guts: especially when they're connected to such a high-profile, public failure that will have real implications for your career. Clearly, Gary Neville should have prepared better for the job, and he admits that, but it was a case of heart ruling head, and those emotions are sometimes so strong they are hard to ignore. It's why people say love is blind and it makes us do stupid things. In a way, when you have opportunities as big as Gary had when he was presented with the Valencia job, it's easy to become distracted from what needs to be done. But I actually don't think Gary should have done anything differently. This was all a massive learning curve, and part of his growth. He hasn't had a managerial job since, but if he did, he'd clearly approach it very differently. Sometimes we need these public failures and visible mistakes, however gut-wrenching they may be, to snap us awake and sort us out. To force us to learn some cold hard truths – and quickly.

And I, like Gary, learned that the hard way, back in 2016.

———

I had joined JOE.co.uk and helped to launch the first ever football TV show made for Facebook Live. It was a huge honour to be part of the team that did that, especially as I was the host of the show, although looking back, I pretty much only got that job because I knew the creative director of the company. But still, I had to be half-decent to be trusted to front such a big project. It was also my first proper TV-presenting gig.

The first few weeks of the show were a bit like preseason training: hard work, but we got through them with very few injuries. Which was amazing, considering former Tottenham legend Ledley King was one of the regular guests each week.

So I was starting to get into my flow, learning how to deliver links without an autocue (I was just working off cue cards, which is way harder) and work with a producer speaking through an earpiece – all things I'd never done before – while also conducting half-interesting football chat in the studio. I was doing a not-terrible job.

And then the Chapecoense tragedy happened …

In late November 2016, a plane carrying the Brazilian football team Chapecoense to the Copa Sudamericana Finals in Medellín, Colombia, crashed just outside the destination airport after running out of fuel. Only six people among the 77 on board survived, three of them players for the team. It was an awful tragedy, and one that brought the entire footballing world to a standstill.

Of course, being a weekly football show, we couldn't *not* reference it, and our producer decided that instead of discussing it meaninglessly, which would have felt crass when it was so fresh, all we would do was sign off our half-hour show with a message of condolence and support for those involved.

For some reason, perhaps because I was trying to impress my colleagues, I decided to memorise the monologue and deliver it live. I spent all week rehearsing it. I'm a stand-up comedian, I told myself, so remembering things is what I do. But when the moment came and we wrapped up that week's show, I was so determined to get this very sensitive message right that nerves and fear got the better of me, and just three or four words in, I lost my place in the monologue.

I heard the producer mutter, 'Oh god' in my ear. That confirmed that I had completely messed up. I had to wing the rest of it, blurting out my condolences – which, of course, were also JOE. co.uk's official condolences – and desperately trying to get to the end without saying completely the wrong thing and causing a diplomatic incident. The end titles rolled, the cameras were turned off, the producer confirmed we were off-air, and everyone shook hands and left the studio for the post-show debrief in the office.

I was crestfallen. I knew I had fucked up and felt I had let the show down, let myself down and, more importantly, let the victims of the crash and their families down, by bumbling my way through a terrible message of support. I had to fight back tears in the debrief, I was so upset and embarrassed. I raced home and turned off my phone, terrified of the deluge of 'WTF was that, Jim?!' messages that were bound to roll in.

Unlike that gig I'd bombed at, this show was watched by thousands of people every Friday. I just knew that most of them would not only be wondering what had happened with the sign-off, but would probably be understandably (and rightly) upset that I had fucked up a very important and sensitive monologue.

But only one person reacted, and that was the producer. 'That wasn't pretty, was it?' he said with a smirk and a twinkle in his eye. He knew I felt terrible about it, but he also knew I would learn from it and that there was nothing more to be done. Most viewers hadn't noticed it, and there were no nasty comments under the video, no trolling, no criticism. Just football fans reacting to talking points as per any of the previous episodes. But that didn't stop me feeling bad about it and learning from it. I made a mental note to always, ALWAYS, read from the cards when relaying any future message of a similar ilk.

This was a failure that the entire world could have seen (had they wanted to watch). In fact, you can still go to the JOE.co.uk Facebook page and watch it now. But, as with a lot of our failings that appear epic and seem to be very much on show, most other people hardly notice them, and life moves on very quickly. And even those errors that are noticed are often accepted anyway. We're all human, and we all make mistakes.

———

The theme of a perceived public failure when others might not have noticed it (although my producer at JOE.co.uk may disagree) is something that *Countdown* legend Susie Dent also touched upon when she was a guest on the *Blank Podcast*. Susie is an incredibly intelligent person, having studied modern languages at Oxford and Princeton, but is not particularly comfortable speaking in front of an audience. However, this is something she has to do on book tours and, of course, in her role as house lexicographer on *Countdown*.

She told us she feels a lot of pressure to be absolutely perfect all the time in her explanations and to have a really good grasp of her subject, as language is her 'thing'. But in her head, she often thinks that she has no idea what she is about to say, or that she doesn't have enough of a handle on what she is talking about. She added that she feels that pressure even in everyday life from her friends, who say they are worried to text her in case their grammar is wrong.

But Susie told us that she had worked on owning that potential for embarrassment, that shame and that vulnerability, and has tried to embrace it – and that's something we can all do in moments of public failure, or in those (sometimes worse) moments when we simply fear failure. The truth is that no one cares about it as much as you do – and before long, it will be over, and everyone will have moved on.

Susie told us she had been reading a lot about facing fears that are stopping you from doing things. She had been telling herself that if something bad happens, no one is going to remember it in a week's time, and those embarrassing moments might actually help you learn something you wouldn't have learned had you been too afraid to try. At the same time, she had learned not to feel like she had to say yes to every interview, especially if she wasn't an authority on the subject.

Vulnerability is part of life and it isn't necessarily a bad thing, so she had decided not to catastrophise all the time, and to remind herself that people have their own things going on and

won't be spending nearly as much time thinking about her bad
moments as she does. That it's okay to let go and say, 'Fuck it,
I don't care' a bit more.

We could all use a little more 'fuck it, I don't care' from time to
time. We all obsess over silly things we have done, but letting
them go is freeing. It feels like a weight off your shoulders to
just let what happens happen and move on. Not to mention the
amount of time you get back by not worrying about it, because
the only person wasting their time thinking about it is you.

What was actually quite reassuring about Susie's admissions
was knowing that this incredibly intelligent person, the sort
of qualified person who usually makes me feel inferior, had
the exact same vulnerabilities and worries that I did. Susie
sharing these worries was really brave of her and was actually
a comfort to me. I really appreciated her in that moment.

———

The freedom of letting go is something that one guest, a TV
presenter, definitely agreed with when we chatted to them –
although, with a more bullish personality than someone like
Susie, they came at it from a different angle. In short, they
had a lot more 'fuck it, I don't care' about them.

They talked about the idea of three concentric circles. The
smallest circle, in the middle, is what's within your control;
then you have the second circle, which is things in your
influence; and the outer circle contains all the things that are
out of your control. If it's out of your control, there's no point
wasting time worrying about it; if it's within your influence,
then there's a point to which you can worry about it, but not
too much; and if it's within your control, it's down to you. I
think this is such a powerful image.

They went on to talk about practising extreme responsibility. This presenter will blame themselves when things go wrong, but *only* if it's actually their fault. If something bad happens that is out of their control – for example, a broadcast shoot goes wrong because of a technical glitch – they let it go immediately. They have no power over it, so obsessing over it is wasted energy. But if they can claim an element of responsibility, however small, they like to focus on that, because it's something they can learn from and change next time. They talked about giving yourself that power to take responsibility. If there's not one little thing you could have done, then fine, you can't kick yourself – but in most situations, you can find something, they explained. You don't want to just brush past it, so you should give yourself 24 hours to feel crap about it. This is part of the process. But by the next day, you should focus on what you could do next time to avoid that failure, and ensure you're not making the same mistake again. You have to feel bad enough to want to change – that was the crux of their message.

I definitely don't need an excuse to kick myself or feel sorry for myself – sometimes it happens without me even making any mistakes. But the idea that a mistake is a process that involves some personal shaming and that it's *good* is an interesting one. That it's good to punish yourself, as long as you learn from it. And that's the key. You can't just hammer yourself after every mistake for weeks on end and then go and make the same error a month later.

It reminds me of some advice, based on comedian Sarah Millican's 11 O'Clock Rule, that was given to me in the early days of doing stand-up. It's about reflection, balance, learning and moving on: 'After every gig, no matter whether it was brilliant or terrible, give yourself until 11 a.m. the next morning to bask or wallow in that. If it was great, let yourself think you're amazing until 11 a.m. If you died on your arse, let yourself feel like an idiot until 11 a.m. Then let it go and move on.'

It clearly worked for Sarah, as she is one of the UK's best-loved and most successful comedians. I've been trying to apply it ever since learning it, and – give or take a few weeks where terrible gigs seemed to follow each other, and that stint away from stand-up – it's a rule that has served me pretty well. I do find it easier to move on after the good gigs than the bad ones, if I'm being totally honest, and maybe that's just human nature – that we focus on the negative. But actually allowing yourself a window to feel those raw emotions before moving on is a helpful part of the process.

And that's what the TV presenter was saying too, about kicking yourself. Don't let yourself off, punish yourself a bit – but make sure you treat that wound with kindness afterwards, and learn from it to make sure you don't do it again. The only thing I would say is that giving yourself until 11 a.m. to wallow might not be so helpful if the mistake happened at 11.01 a.m. the previous day!

I think this brutal approach does also mean asking the question 'Why have I failed?' If we ask ourselves that, we can go some way towards working out what not to do in the future. My failures mentioned in this chapter nearly all boil down to a lack of preparation and experience. I know I would have been better and done better in both situations had I prepared for them better. For the TV gaffe, for example, had I thought ahead and acknowledged that I may stumble over my words, I could have asked the director to put a still image on screen – the Chapecoense badge for example – thereby allowing me to look at my card and read the monologue verbatim. For the gig where I died, if I had been gigging more consistently, I would have performed much better on the night and wouldn't have been so rusty. And if I had been writing more in between gigs, I probably would have had better material to fall back on.

None of these are ground-breaking ideas, but it took me having some very embarrassing public failures to realise what I was

34 doing wrong, and to make sure that, going forward, I avoided similar scenarios. And I'm delighted to announce that, since then, both my television appearances and gigs have been much more successful. I just needed to be able to kick myself for a bit and then learn from my mistakes.

Chapter 2:
Imposter Syndrome

When I first moved to London, I really felt out of my depth and I think one thing that just took me a while was asking for help and talking to people about how you feel ... I get imposter syndrome quite a lot, but we all had those close people, it could be like a group of people or friends or could be one person that can just be honest with you.

Laura Whitmore

Most of us, at one time or another, have experienced being in a situation where we feel like we aren't good enough, like we're frauds and there must be someone far better qualified to do whatever it is we're doing.

When actor John Bradley came on the *Blank Podcast*, he spoke about how the type of performance he wants to give is always about getting as much out of every single second as he can. It's not just about learning the lines, it's also the physical aspects. He explained that he tries to inject as much colour into his performance as he can. But in doing that, you can sometimes create problems for yourself, because you don't really *have* to do that and sometimes it's much simpler (and easier) to just tell the story.

For John, he thinks it's to do with being working class – that for him, it's some kind of inferiority complex because he feels he shouldn't really be there. For this reason, he pushes himself even harder than most people would. It's imposter syndrome, really ... he always works as hard as he can to convince people they've made the right choice when casting him.

Imposter syndrome (or imposter phenomenon, as it is sometimes called) was first identified in the 1970s by psychologists Pauline Rose Clance and Suzanne Imes, who theorised that, at times, we believe we are inadequate and incompetent, despite evidence that indicates quite the opposite to be true.

I recently tweeted asking others to sum up in one word what imposter syndrome meant to them. I was amazed by the number of people who responded, and also by the many words that came up time and time again, such as *fraud, insecure, scary, unqualified, inadequacy, anxiety, self-doubt, faker* and *unworthy*.

Indeed, for me, all those words have applied while we've been making this podcast. I have had many moments of feeling like I was the wrong person for the job, and that my limited abilities and experience would be brought to the fore. Sitting down with so many incredibly successful people is inspiring and intimidating in equal measure.

Although these feelings of inadequacy have so far failed to deter me from continuing this project, I must admit that, each time a new episode drops, that impending-doom sense that I am properly shit at hosting and producing a podcast and am about to get found out looms heavy in my mind. In fact, I know that when I read these words back before sending them to our editor, I'll be thinking, 'They'll never publish this pile of chaff.' (Readers might be expressing similar thoughts at this point.)

It's fair to say that imposter syndrome affects most aspects of my creative life – whether it's writing an article or playing a riff, I never quite feel like I'm confident in my abilities or accomplishments, and then my stomach starts to churn and the butterflies appear. What has been a stark (and positive) reality check for me while doing the *Blank Podcast* has been how many of our guests feel the same as I do, and how prevalent imposter syndrome is among creative people. Even the most successful people in the world will have had those moments. Just think about actress Jodie Foster after she won an Academy Award for her performance in *The Accused*, when she described how she expected people to come knocking on her door to take the award back, saying, 'Excuse me, we meant to give that to … Meryl Streep.'

The first time we really discussed this topic on the podcast was with actress Amanda Abbington, and she really nailed how I often feel myself. Amanda talked about how she often thinks of herself as a bit of a mongrel instead of a pedigree in acting terms, and that she doesn't know whether that's stood her in good stead or been a hindrance. It's a mindset that has left her feeling a little bit out of her depth at times, particularly in situations like press nights at a theatre. She told us it's in those moments she really feels like she's a fake, yet she knows it's not because she's a bad actor or that she can't do the job. It's more about having to blow your own trumpet, and instead of doing that and being confident about a performance, Amanda often ends up apologising.

THE TURING TEST

In 1950, the English mathematician and computer scientist Alan Turing proposed a test that evaluated a machine's ability to exhibit intelligent behaviour that was equivalent to or indistinguishable from that of a human. It led to much speculation and debate around the idea that computers could be as intelligent as humans.

BLANK

The test itself involved a human evaluator sending a series of written questions to a computer and another human, and receiving answers from each in return. If the person asking the questions could not distinguish between human and computer in the answers, then it was deemed that the computer was intelligent.

Some 40 years on, in the 1990s, sociologist Harry Collins started to use the test to prove a theory later dubbed 'interactional expertise'. Collins's studies included seeing whether, for example, participants who were colour-blind could pass as not colour-blind, or whether participants without perfect pitch could pass as being able to recognise musical notes, and vice versa.

The results were incredibly interesting and followed patterns whereby those who had colour-blindness were better able to pass for those who did not, whereas participants who were not colour-blind found it much harder to pass as if they were. Curiously, those with perfect pitch were better able to emulate those without perfect pitch. What became clear is that other factors are at play – language, for one, being a strong descriptor that guides other senses, which might explain why it's easier to hide that you're colour-blind.

Collins himself decided to see if he could test his theory by passing himself off as a physicist. Having spent years hanging around and talking shop with many physicists, he thought he had garnered enough expertise to convince other people. To test this, he answered seven questions about gravity-wave physics, and his replies – along with answers to the same questions from a real gravitational physicist – were sent to nine experts in the field. Out of those nine judges, seven couldn't decide and two chose Collins as the physicist.

What Collins's experiments go to show is that by talking to and interacting with our peers and mentors, we can help ourselves feel better about our level of knowledge and skill. Turing's test is also called the 'imitation game', but when it comes to our own imposter syndrome, we need to acknowledge that the moments in which we experience the feeling that we are winging it – that we have no authority – are a time of discovery and learning, and that imitation is just a means to an end.

———

This idea of curating our own identities so we can avoid those moments of falling victim to imposter syndrome is something Dawn French alluded to when she talked on the podcast about her time as a young exchange student in New York.

Dawn knew she was going to America, and during the process of selecting where to go, she had to fill out a form saying where she'd like to live, if given the choice. At that point, Dawn was a real country girl who rode horses, and she'd never lived in the city. So her first choice was Oklahoma, and she was imagining big saddles, mustangs and cowboys … that's what she envisaged America to be. But because every other kid had put New York as their first choice, perversely, they sent Dawn to New York and gave all the other kids placements in Oklahoma. This upset Dawn, as all she knew of New York was from gritty cop shows like *Kojak*, and she saw the city as the sort of place where you might get murdered. But something struck her as she got on the plane with her little bag and the money her mum and dad had saved up for her: she realised that all the people she was about to meet didn't know her, so she could be anything. She decided she was going to be confident, funny, sharp and popular – she was going to be like a New Yorker. She admitted that keeping up such a pretence was exhausting at times, but, by faking that kind of confidence, you can kind of catch up to it and create your own confidence. Eventually, that confidence really did belong to her.

BLANK

———

Often when we're in the middle of doing something, our inner narrative starts to take over, and any outside voices can feel disruptive and unhelpful. And that can even be true when it comes to receiving compliments, in a way that can sometimes exacerbate the feeling that we aren't worthy and hinder our ability to acknowledge our successes.

One comedian was really candid when they came on the podcast and told us how they really can't bear getting compliments, especially within the first half hour of coming off stage. They recalled a preview show they had, one they say was probably one of the best gigs in their entire life. Within 20 minutes of coming off stage, a friend was saying the loveliest things and something inside them just went 'meh'. They hated it and they felt crushed, and so they started questioning themselves: 'What's wrong with me? Why am I sabotaging these compliments?' For them, those moments after performing are a really fragile time. What they said resonated with me, and it definitely made me think about how to approach my feelings in those moments going forward.

When Gary Neville was on, he mentioned how, at a time when he was dealing with lots of negative thoughts, he sought the advice of a psychologist to figure out a way of getting a handle on both negative and positive comments.

The psychologist got Gary to consider how, if he woke up in the morning feeling happy, he'd be in a positive frame of mind and would work really hard that day, but if he then read something negative in the newspaper or someone shouted at him from the other side of the street, all of a sudden that earlier positivity might become negativity. Gary questioned the absurdity of this – that you've worked for thousands of hours, you've given all your life to football, and you're going to let something written in a paper or someone shouting at you affect your whole outlook. That example helped to simplify things for him, even to the point where he tries to resist praise. He feels that if you're able to discard both excessive criticism and praise, you can turn down the noise and hopefully level yourself out.

A little modesty is never a bad thing, of course, but many of us choose to react negatively to feedback so regularly that it becomes second nature, and we put too much trust in this mindset and that of others who might be doing the same thing.

For me, imposter syndrome strikes in one of two different ways. Sometimes, it's like someone tiptoeing up behind me, putting their hands over my eyes and whispering 'Guess who?' into my ear; and other times, it's like a bruising smack in the face. Each of them jars me in equal measure.

In the early episodes of the *Blank Podcast*, something that began to be a bit of a catchphrase for Jim was 'giving ourselves the wins' – the idea being that, far too often, we are so hard on ourselves that we don't enjoy our achievements, and it's when we change the script internally that we can start to be more at ease with the situation. Changing the script in my own mind has been no simple task, but when meeting guests for the first time and listening to their own experiences, it's now less, 'They're going to find me out, I'm no good at this,' and more, 'It's okay, new experiences bring new challenges and learning, and it just takes time, but you'll get there.'

Because we're all winging it to some degree, we all have these moments, so when they inevitably occur, we just need to remember that we are not, and never will be, alone.

JIM

Imposter syndrome can affect pretty much anyone. And that may sound weird, but far more people have doubted themselves than you think. Famous, not famous, rich, poor, tall, small – whoever. Everyone, at some point, has thought they are a complete fraud.

Well, almost everyone. I tried to think of anyone who never struggled with imposter syndrome, and the only people I could think of were Muhammad Ali, Ali Dia (more on him later) and Cristiano Ronaldo. And even Ronaldo must have had doubts over that haircut when he first joined Manchester United in 2003. But anyway, the point is that imposter syndrome doesn't care how successful or admired you are; it will, at some point, make you think you are well out of your depth.

Having trained as a journalist and then moved into comedy and TV presenting, I have had countless moments of feeling like a fraud and an imposter. But there is one that sticks out, from my early days as a local news reporter.

I was a year out of university with a degree that was awarded to me by a different university because mine hadn't yet been granted the status to be able to officially award degrees – which should have been a warning sign that this was going to be harder than it looked. And it already looked fucking impossible.

But I was desperate to be a reporter. My first job was at the (now defunct) *Uckfield Courier*, covering the patch of Uckfield, a sleepy town in East Sussex. Trying to fill 15 pages with news from a town where nothing happened was like drawing blood from a stone. I prayed for village fetes, I visualised cake sales, I did rain dances so that Uckfield would flood (which it did, but two years before I arrived at the paper – the number of times I was shown photos of people going down the high street in boats …).

So, each week I would ring up various councillors and contacts around town and beg them to tell me something interesting enough to be written up in 250 words, and then hope they could take a decent photo and send it to me so I wouldn't have to ask one of the oddball photographers at the paper to go and do it.

One day, desperate for news, I saw something about a meeting of the local NHS Trust about something or other (I genuinely can't remember what), and my editor thought it might make a decent story, so I was dispatched to Lewes Hospital. When I got there, I was ushered into an office with two men in suits and sat down at a table brimming with paperwork, feeling like I was about to be interviewed for a job. They ran through what felt like hours of medical jargon and references to local government things that I didn't know about because I still hadn't passed any of my NCTJ (National Council for the Training of Journalists) exams. I sat there letting all these words wash over me, desperately hoping for a fire alarm – or even an actual fire.

I'd felt this helpless just once before, and that was during my AS-Level PE exam a few years earlier, when I hadn't bothered revising, assuming that because I was good at football, I'd know it all anyway, only to open the exam paper and realise I couldn't answer a single question, as it was all about physiology rather than football, funnily enough. I just had to sit there in silence. But because I was now in a position of (relative) authority as a local reporter, this felt worse. I should have known some of what they were talking about, but I didn't understand a single thing.

So I smiled and nodded, took notes and blagged my way through it, before being ushered out, not entirely sure what had just happened or what the fuck I was going to write about for the story. I went back to my car and just cried my eyes out, overwhelmed by a sense of helplessness and feeling like a fraud. I was convinced I was going to let down myself, my editor and the fucking East Sussex NHS Trust. But, as with nearly everything connected to imposter syndrome, it was nowhere near as bad as I thought it was going to be.

My editor had basically forgotten about the story by the time I got back to the office, so I didn't have to write it (I just mumbled something about there not being much of a story in it and she seemed satisfied with that). Word eventually got back from the suits in the meeting that I was pleasant and they had enjoyed 'working' with me, and a few months later, I had started to gain more confidence in the role and realised that asking questions wasn't just a good conversation starter, but was also a fundamental part of my job.

Looking back on this makes me realise that imposter syndrome is intrinsically linked to public failure, in that we never really fail as badly as we think, and that other people don't see us as imposters in the way that we see ourselves – in fact, they're usually too wrapped up in their own issues to notice or care what we're doing.

If we are as down on ourselves externally as we are internally, then we set the narrative and other people will follow suit, but if we don't make it obvious, then we let them decide – and 99 times out of 100, they will never be as critical about you as you are about yourself.

Imagine a film critic sitting on a sofa absolutely slamming the movie they're watching on TV, but the movie is your life and the only person watching the show is you. If no one else is watching the show, then they won't pick up on the narrative. You're the critic. *Inception* this ain't!

Anyway, by the time I left the *Uckfield Courier* a year later and moved to one of the company's flagship publications in Sevenoaks, I was – despite that NHS Trust meeting debacle – being hailed as one of the brightest young reporters in the company (even though I still hadn't passed half of my NCTJ prelims, including the one about local government – which, of course, NHS Trusts fall under). I'd never told anyone how low I felt about that meeting, and thus no one had assumed I'd screwed up – and now my career was gaining momentum. Oh, and the *Uckfield Courier* ceased publication just as I left because numbers were at an all-time low, but I'm taking the win, okay?

———

Proving that imposter syndrome affects anyone and everyone is something that came up when *Game of Thrones* actor John Bradley joined us on the *Blank Podcast*, as we've already talked about. He really did worry about people noticing his mistakes – although Susie Dent would no doubt suggest that they probably aren't even thinking about that, and have their own stuff going on that they're worrying about!

John's words here did strike a chord with me, I'll admit. Especially the bit about trying to be the very best you can be every single time. For me, that's certainly linked to imposter syndrome and the feeling that the Fraud Police are going to knock on my door any second now, drag me out into the street, and condemn me for being absolutely terrible while all my friends and neighbours watch. But trying to be the absolute best every time you do whatever it is you do is tiring. It is so very tiring. And it's not even really possible. Can anyone perform at maximum capacity all the time? Of course not! But for some reason, many of us – especially those of us in creative industries – feel we have to be on our game every single time.

The truth is, you don't. Listening to John talk about the mental and physical pain he's gone through (to the point of developing a real-life stutter for a part) made me realise that no job is worth ruining your life for. John went on to say precisely that on the podcast, and told us he's made peace with himself and his performances, and this made me look more kindly on my own creative work.

Is it brilliant all the time? Hell no! But when those brilliant days come around, do I accept them, and maybe even enjoy them a little? Well, I'm certainly trying to ...

THE STRANGE CASE OF ALI DIA

Speak to any English football fan and they will be able to tell you exactly who Ali Dia is, even though his professional career amounted to only 58 minutes.

Dia was a 31-year-old journeyman semi-professional footballer with a fairly unspectacular track record who was, frankly, not that good. But he somehow managed to convince decorated footballer and manager Graeme Souness, who was in charge of Premier League side Southampton, to literally let him play for the Saints, one of England's oldest professional clubs. And not just in a friendly or charity match, but an actual Premier League game. It was like Giles or me playing for ... well, Southampton. He was, of course, pretty terrible. As any of us non-Premier League footballers would be. It took Souness less than an hour to realise he'd been scammed, and he hauled Dia off.

But it was an hour too long, and by then the story had exploded. Southampton star Matt Le Tissier later described Dia as 'Bambi on ice', and pundits, fans, commentators and former footballers all jumped at the chance to lambast the Saints for being duped and playing this faker. Twenty-four years later, the story is still talked about as one of the craziest moments in English football.

The way Dia had managed to earn himself a game was perhaps even stranger. It transpired he had convinced a friend to call Souness pretending to be George Weah, Africa's most famous player, claiming to be Dia's cousin and recommending him to the Saints. Weah at that time was at the height of his career – he was playing for Italian giants AC Milan and had just been crowned the world's best player. It was a bold move on Dia's part and was also not true at all.

Without the internet and the ability to fact-check as quickly and thoroughly as we do now, Souness and Southampton allowed Dia to play after just one day of training – in which, presumably, he didn't look too terrible. Either that, or Souness and his staff just weren't paying attention.

It turned out many years later that the incredibly average footballer Dia had been using the Weah lie to wrangle his way into a multitude of semi-professional and professional-but-not-that-great clubs in Scandinavia, Germany and the lower English leagues. Each time he turned up, played pretty badly and left after a handful of games, only to rock up somewhere else thanks to the George Weah hoax.

Southampton were by far the biggest club he managed to dupe, and the legend of Dia's scam will forever be told – though Souness, famously a gruff individual who doesn't suffer fools, has rarely spoken publicly about it, as few have been brave enough to ask him.

But where this tale relates to imposter syndrome is that Dia, in the few times he has been tracked down by journalists since, appears to have absolutely zero regrets and no sense of imposter syndrome. He turned up at non-league side Gateshead after Southampton, a drop of five divisions, and told the *Gateshead Post*: 'I have been portrayed as a con man and a poor player, but I am neither and intend to prove people wrong. Obviously I'm disappointed not to have made it in the Premiership, but I've got faith in my own ability and my only concern now is Gateshead. My contract is just until the end of the season. But if things go well, who knows, I could stay longer.'

If things go well? You've just been exposed on a national level as a complete fraud and charlatan and a not very good footballer! But clearly, Dia didn't care. He would even smile when he was subbed off in games.

Jim Platt, Dia's manager at Gateshead, told Bleacher Report: 'He wasn't a bad fella. He was quite personable. Even when I took him off, he just smiled … Other players would have just told me to fuck off.'

This was a guy for whom the phrase 'imposter syndrome' clearly did not register, even though he was 100 per cent a bona fide imposter. He was literally described as an imposter in many of the national newspapers, but it seemed to have little or no effect on his confidence. If anything, it improved it! He actually went on to score two goals in eight games for Gateshead before disappearing off the face of the earth.

As ridiculous as this story is, I think there is something to take away from it. That, actually, ignorance is bliss. We suffer from imposter syndrome because we overthink and we overanalyse ourselves and everyone around us. Ali Dia didn't. He just got on with it. Even though the thing he was getting on with was something he was very bad at.

There is a very good chance that you will be better at the thing you are trying to do than Ali Dia was at football, so you deserve to ignore your imposter syndrome much more than he did. Being ignorant of his own limitations got Dia to the Premier League. Ignoring your imposter syndrome could get you even further. He didn't see what he did as a scam or cheating, he just did what he could to get to the top. Okay, his moment at the top lasted 58 minutes, but he still got there. I actually think we could all be a bit more like Ali Dia in our lives and our careers, and the results could be spectacular!

We are often the first to deny ourselves the opportunities we deserve. Probably because we don't think we deserve them or we can't see them happening even when they are right in front of us. But who's to say we don't deserve them? Most people would probably think we do. Enough people clearly thought Dia deserved a go, as he kept getting offered deals.

Dia may not have had the skill, but he did, for some reason, have the confidence. Now, imagine mixing that confidence with someone actually quite good at their job (i.e. you), and think how much of a difference that could make. Let's all be a bit more Ali Dia from now on.

———

From one footballer to another, although they're not really comparable in any way at all ...

Gary Lineker is England's third all-time top scorer and one of the most iconic footballers in the world, despite having been retired for almost three decades. He also fronts BBC's flagship football round-up show, *Match of the Day*, and is seen as a role model for many young players due to his work ethic, success, and image as football's nice guy. For example, in a 16-year playing career, he was never booked, not even once! But, strangely, for a man who is viewed by many to be England's greatest-ever striker, Gary told us he didn't feel he was any good at scoring goals until he was 26.

It was during a game for England in the mid-1980s, almost a decade after he'd made his professional debut for Leicester City, during which time he'd scored plenty of goals. Now playing for Barcelona, Lineker scored a hat-trick against arch rivals Real Madrid – in the game known in Spain as El Clásico – and a couple of weeks later, went one better and scored four for the Three Lions against his adopted homeland Spain in a friendly. Jogging back to the halfway line after the fourth goal, feeling in a state of shock, he said to teammate Bryan Robson, 'I don't know why this is happening, I'm so lucky,' to which the England captain replied, 'Oh, eff off, you,' though in slightly harsher language. It was in that moment that Lineker thought: 'Oh, I'm actually good at this: I'm good at scoring goals.'

Prior to that game, he had always had the fear that somehow he would be found out, that the game of football would catch up with him, but it never did. He had confidence because you need confidence to survive in the environment of football, but clearly it was slightly faked. However, those words from Robson snapped him out of it.

That fear, though, kept him grounded, Gary admitted. That and the fact that, by the time he really got going in his professional career, he wasn't that young. He was 21 when he started to play regular football in a Leicester side that was yo-yoing between the top two divisions in England. Compared to the likes of Michael Owen, who was 17 when he was thrust into the limelight at Liverpool – as well as countless teenage stars who are all fireworks when they start but burn out not long after – Lineker's career was a gradual process. He thinks that is what gave his career its longevity: he was able to grow up and learn about being a footballer. He avoided the issues many young footballers have these days, like having to make big life decisions at a very young age (or having people around you who make the wrong decisions for you).

I have to admit I was gobsmacked when Gary told us he didn't consider himself good at scoring goals until he was 26. By the time of that Clásico in January 1987, he had scored 171 career goals in 309 games for club and country.*

I totally understand getting to 26 and still not having worked out what your thing is. I definitely felt that way and I think a lot of people feel the same – certainly in the creative industries. And Gary is absolutely right that in the world of high-level sport, in any category, fans do expect a lot from very young people, and that is something I will never quite understand. In the creative world, fans seem to let you develop at your own pace, but in sport, the demand for success is intense and immediate. That can put an incredible amount of pressure on an athlete's mind, and it is why, sadly, you hear countless stories about young footballers suffering from depression and having other problems when their careers don't work out in the way they (and others) had hoped.

---

* https://www.transfermarkt.co.uk/gary-lineker/leistungsdatendetails/ spieler/22256/plus/0/saison/1986/wettbewerb/ES1/verein/131/https://www. englandstats.com/matches.php?mid= 622) (For those of you keeping score, his record was 175 goals in 316 games by the time the clock hit 90 minutes in that Spain friendly in February.)

So it was refreshing to hear Gary talk so honestly about his struggle with imposter syndrome, despite being one of the best in the world at his thing at the time, but it was also true that he had needed to accept his greatness. We all do. So find your own Bryan Robson to tell you to shut up and accept your greatness. It might just help you flourish.

———

The thing that always helps ground me when I'm feeling like a complete fraud is to try to notice how other people describe me. I won't have told them how to describe me, so if they say I am one thing then I must be. If someone says I am friendly – well then, that's their experience of me, so I guess I must be. If someone says I am creative, they must have seen me do something creative, so yeah, I guess I probably am. If someone says I am good-looking, I know they're lying.

When I was younger, I hated the idea of being tall for some unknown reason, but people kept telling me I was 'at least six foot'. 'No way, I'm five-ten max,' I'd say. Again, I have no idea why I was so adamant about not being tall – hey, I was a weird kid. But every time I measured myself, there it was, clear as day on the wall: bang on six foot.

For ages, I cringed when people called me a comedian. Like they must have been thinking, 'Oh my god, does he think he is a comedian? What a fraud!'

'I can't be,' I said to myself. 'I don't have an agent, I don't really gig that much, I'm not even really that funny.' But people would refer to me as a comedian, and seemingly in a serious way. 'They don't know,' I'd tell myself. 'They don't know how hard it is to be a comedian, and I haven't earned it yet, so I'll let them think that, but deep down I know I'm not a comedian.' Even though the one thing I wanted more than anything in life was to be a comedian. I was committing self-sabotage via imposter syndrome.

Then I got an agent. A real-life comedy agent. Even then, I thought, 'They've made a mistake here. They think I'm someone else.' But the contracts came through, they had my name on, I signed them and then I was on their website. 'They'll work it out eventually,' I thought.

Then we had comedy legend David Baddiel come on the *Blank Podcast*. He and Frank Skinner's legendary *Fantasy Football League* was one of the reasons I became a comedian. I would tape it and watch it over and over again as a kid – a kid who didn't realise he was setting himself up for a life in comedy decades later.

During the podcast, David turned to me, while talking about being a comedian and said, 'Jim, you're a comedian, aren't you?'

I thought, 'Well, shit. If David freaking Baddiel thinks I'm a comedian, then I probably am one! Who am I to argue with David Baddiel?' And the thing is, labelling myself as a comedian, or being labelled as a comedian, didn't mean that I'd finally made it. Of course I hadn't. No one had ever fucking heard of me!

But it did mean that imposter syndrome is wrong. I *am* a comedian. I may not be a successful comedian, I may not be a busy comedian – hell, I may not even be a particularly good comedian – but I am one. And if you don't agree, take it up with David Baddiel.

Chapter 3:
Grief

A good mantra is 'the only way out is through' and it is so true. If you try to side-step stuff it just gets bigger. Whenever I have blanked, I just think: head straight in the shit. And oh god it's horrible, but there's that element of me that just goes 'right let's have it'. If you visit it, everything else afterwards is such a relief.

Dawn French

Grief is a state of mind so many of us find ourselves in throughout our lives, when loss brings with it pain that can feel like it will never truly heal. We all experience it in a unique way, and there is no universal way of dealing with it.

Sitting down to write this is extremely significant for me personally, as it's 36 years to the day that my mum, Brenda, passed away from leukaemia. Grief is very difficult to define, but for me it is a feeling of intense sadness and yearning – a yearning not only for the person who is no longer there, but also for the lost moments we should have shared with that person: wedding days, births of children, Christmases, and, of course, those times when things aren't going so well for us, those blank moments that this book is about, in which that person would have been a shoulder to cry on or someone to turn to. Those are the moments I often yearn for – as well as simply to be able to talk to the person who knew me best of all.

Grief is, above all, a titanic juggernaut of chaos thundering through our everyday lives, and what is left in its wake is change – massive, incomprehensible change. Many on the fringe of the situation perceive grief as having a finite time frame, like there is a use-by-date for getting back to normal and then our recovery will be complete. But grief, for so many of us, is like a ghost that continues to haunt us for our entire lives.

From my own experience, loss has become a huge part of who I am and what I do, and it's something I've written and talked about extensively. When Dame Kelly Holmes came on to the podcast, we talked at length about the impact the death of her mother had on her life, and continues to have moving forwards.

She told us how she cried every day for three weeks, until her mum was finally buried, and how she felt in such a mess that even leaving the house and being with other people became extremely challenging, because if someone didn't know she'd just lost her mum, they might ask for an autograph, or if they did know what had happened, they would ask how she was or say they were sorry for her loss – and for Kelly this was just so painful to hear. So, for several weeks, she just cocooned herself in her house and only saw close friends and family, and at times this was a great comfort. Kelly described those moments as very special, because being able to open up and talk to others helped her to cope with that period of her life.

Grief can often leave its sufferers feeling hollow and empty, as they are deprived of a loved one and that person's love and affection. These feelings can lead to moments of loneliness, heartache and sometimes despair, because a piece of you is missing. Loneliness is sometimes equated with physically being alone, but some of my loneliest moments have been in the company of others, particularly if I need to talk about my grief but they find the subject a difficult one to tackle.

Being able to talk about subjects like grief and share your feelings is so powerful, and the podcast has allowed me to hear other people's experiences and connect to other people's stories. When the subject of grief comes up during our conversations on the podcast, I have found, time and time again, that the best response is empathy. An experience in common – a shared loneliness, even – becomes a uniting moment in which to allow someone else in and to support each other, and to listen to and learn from what grief means to them.

When we spoke to Stephen Mangan, he told us about the death of his mum, and how much it motivated him to identify and pursue the things he wanted to do in life. He said that by the time he'd finished his degree, he still didn't really know what he was going to do, and then his mum became very ill with cancer and he made the decision to stay at home and look after her for a year. She died aged just 45, and knowing that his maternal grandmother had also died of cancer at a similar age, a notion formed in Stephen's head that he might only have 20 more years to live – so why not try being an actor?

Stephen described his mum's illness as changing his life in more ways than one. There was grief, of course, but it also made him think, 'I'll give this a go.' The loss triggered an internal stopwatch – time became a precious thing and he sought to make the most of his circumstances. It propelled him to figure out and pursue the career he wanted – in fact it was probably the defining moment for him in becoming an actor – and it's a reminder of where he has come from and where he still wants to go.

The phrase 'life is short' is a cliché but it's also true, and it makes me think of those I've lost. In my own creative life, I have always believed that I need to make the most of the time I've got. Although I will not live forever, I want to make stuff that will – and that will give me the opportunity to convey my own experiences of loss, just as artists have been doing for hundreds of years.

THE ART OF GRIEVING

A 15-century work by the painter Hans Memling entitled *Triptych of Earthly Vanity and Divine Salvation* is a prime example of a visceral depiction of an artist's feelings around mortality. Consisting of six oil paintings on wooden panels, the front side features a naked woman flanked by Death and the Devil surrounded by flames. Grisly, evocative and unusually erotic for the time, the piece juxtaposes the earthly sin of life and hollow pain of death.

Art, in all its many forms – whether it be painting, writing, filmmaking or music – allows both the creator and the consumer

When we create, we give ourselves permission to examine all that is happening within our grieving bodies.

Douglas Mitchell, therapist

to address topics often seen as taboo. Art enables us to see things differently and sometimes even universally.

In 2011, the Taiwanese-American artist Candy Chang painted the wall of a building in New Orleans with chalkboard paint and wrote a simple message over and over again – 'Before I die I want to _____' – the idea being that passers-by would fill in the end of the sentence. In the next 24 hours, something truly remarkable occurred, and the wall filled up with a huge selection of people's personal messages, hopes and dreams.

The inspiration for this piece came from Chang's own experience of loss after a friend died; it was a chance for her to reflect on the pain she was feeling and find kinship with others. Social media allowed the story to spread like wildfire, and copycat pieces started popping up all over the world. In fact, the demand became so great that Chang created a toolkit for others, including stencils that can be downloaded so people can create their own walls.

In an interview, Chang said of the project: 'Our public spaces are our shared spaces and at their greatest, they can help us make sense of the beauty and tragedy of life with the people around us.' Since that first wall, over 5,000 'Before I Die …' pieces have been created in more than 175 countries, proving that art speaks to so many of us.

———

Grief often has a way of informing our lives and gives us the opportunity to reflect on a situation we might see no way out of. Presenter Jake Humphrey spoke to us about his grandmother, who took her own life, and how during a dark time in his life, he thought about her death and how that had created a weird relationship with suicide for him. It was something he had

BLANK

spoken to his family about back when his grandma died, and
the message that stayed with him from that discussion was
that they felt that killing yourself shows you're actually strong
enough to live. Hearing that meant that when Jake went through
a very difficult period in his twenties, suicide was not an option
because of that message – that if someone can do that, then
they are strong enough to live. When he spoke to us, ten years
on from his grandma's death, Jake revealed this thought had
probably saved his life.

Grief as a teacher is something I've only recently come to think
about, and while the lessons are incredibly painful and the
burden of knowledge is long-lasting, it is never insignificant.
For me, loss has had a huge influence on my personality – I
take little for granted, I'm always aware things can change in
an instant, I stay in the present and appreciate things in the
moment, and I rarely look too far ahead. Grief has made me
who I am. It's made me spontaneous, creative, compassionate,
paranoid, anxious; there is so much of me that is informed by
my experiences of loss.

Writing this chapter has been such a challenge for me. Grief is
a subject that I am so close to – too close, perhaps – and it has
been a constant presence in my creative life, from song lyrics to
novels to magazine articles I've written. My own blank moments
have often come when grief is something I have to focus on,
for example writing my book *One Hundred and Fifty-Two Days*,
which focuses on my experiences with losing my mum, often left
me feeling blank and empty. But our weekly podcast recordings,
which Jim and I often refer to as 'therapy sessions', have
lessened these feelings, and writing this today I do feel a sense
of comfort in the thought that every time I take that leap, the
landing grows ever softer.

We all deal with grief in different ways, and we all grieve for different things. I've grieved for lost grandparents and friends just like anyone else. Each time it happens is different from the others, because each person means something different to me.

But we don't just grieve for people. Losing a possession that means something to you, losing a job that you love, losing an opportunity you really want – all these things can result in a grieving process that has as much of a profound effect on you as losing a person you loved.

Game of Thrones star John Bradley spoke on the podcast about grieving for lost work, after his eight-year stint as Samwell Tarly on the HBO series came to an end. It was like he was losing a friend, and losing a part of himself, too. He felt like he was abandoning the character and getting off the bus early, and he wanted to see what was going to happen next for Sam. Even now John misses him, even though playing Sam was often a tough process, and the role took him to some painful places as an actor. The fact that Sam finished the *Game of Thrones* story in a happier place (no spoilers!) was something that John appreciated. He had clearly built up a close relationship with his character, and ending that was hard for him.

Jobs are so weird, because they can become all-consuming and mean so much to you, even if you don't want them to, or don't realise they do. John's analogy of getting off the bus early is so painfully spot on, and it reminds me of the biggest loss I've ever felt after a job – which was the biggest job of my career at that point – and the grieving process I went through after losing it. I didn't understand it was grief until a few years later, but it was such a gut punch that it affected me in ways I didn't even realise – and, in a way, it still does today.

BLANK

The job was the aforementioned JOE.co.uk presenting gig, which was a five-month whirlwind of learning on the go, creative successes and failures, and a mental health rollercoaster. In many ways, that one job encompassed several issues we cover in this book, and I find that almost every episode of the podcast we record relates back to that job in some way. I've never really spoken publicly about it, as there's always a worry in the creative industries that you might be slagging off the wrong person, burning bridges or generally coming across as an ungrateful idiot, so I won't be naming anyone here – but there is a specific episode that relates to this chapter and it's something that I need to get off my chest (which I have also done many times in counselling).

First, a bit of backstory: at the time I got the job I was a semi-professional stand-up comedian and a very inexperienced presenter. Now I think about it, I'm not even sure I'd done any presenting at all, aside from bits on YouTube – which I remember bigging up massively during my interview. In fact, I took the Ali Dia approach to my job application and interview, and I actually concluded my cover letter with the phrase: 'If you hire me, you are hiring a legend.' I'd never done anything like that before – and haven't since – but I was so convinced I wasn't going to get the job (imposter syndrome coming into play there) that I just went for it, assuming nothing would happen. I did also know the managing director at JOE.co.uk at the time, who was reviewing the job applications, and he knew enough about me to know that line was in jest – but even so, it was a pretty bold thing to say!

Incredibly, I got the interview, and even more incredibly, I got the job. Whether they saw something in me or whether it was just my mate in a position of power singing my praises, I'll never know. It obviously helps massively in this industry to know people in certain positions like that, and I'd imagine at least half of on-air jobs go to people who are mates with the people casting them. Probably more.

But I didn't care – it was a big job for me, and the most money I'd ever earned in a full-time role. And creatively, it was a big opportunity. They specifically brought me on board to capitalise on my creativity. They wanted me to host and produce a weekly football show alongside a producer brought in from BT Sport; they wanted me to write and perform comedy sketches; and they wanted me to work with their other creatives to come up with and star in live, pranky viral videos on Facebook (which I was less enthused about). It was a massive confidence boost to get the job, and it was incredibly exciting to get going. JOE.co.uk had a huge platform, and getting the chance to work with others at a proper production company and see my ideas come to life was so exciting. It was almost like I'd won Willy Wonka's Golden Ticket, and was somehow now living this dream of doing whatever I wanted, with the support of these established people.

To cut a long story short, what I discovered fairly quickly was that, through no fault of their own, no one on the editorial and creative teams had much of an idea of what was expected from them or what to do. Office meetings and subsequent instructions quickly became incredibly complicated and confusing, and there was plenty of moaning around the coffee machine as a result. There was zero feedback on ideas from anyone high up, and this led to everything becoming much messier than it needed to be and resulted in a general lack of direction. I often went home feeling terrible about myself and my work – that I'd not done what they wanted and that I was failing big-time after being given this incredible opportunity, although I wasn't quite sure how or why I was failing, because no one was telling me anything. I just assumed I was.

Some ideas worked and some didn't, which of course is the nature of online content. When things worked, the mood about the place was like we'd just landed a rocket on the moon rather than achieved one million views on Facebook. When things failed, the office felt like a football changing room after a cup final defeat. What we were doing meant everything and nothing, all at the same time.

After about two months, I wanted to leave. I would come home and moan to my wife about it all and vow to just quit and do my own thing, although I knew I didn't have anywhere near the online presence to do that, and we needed the money. What was most frustrating was that I asked for feedback all the time, but I never got any. Just empty platitudes and vague statements. Never praise, never constructive criticism – which I absolutely craved because I wanted to prove myself. I sort of felt like a dead man walking, like they didn't want to give me any feedback because I'd be out the door soon anyway. And as it turned out, that was exactly the case.

Even the way I was dispatched was feebly done. I was told in early December that the football show was taking a break after failing to secure a sponsor. It was stressed that this was nothing to do with my performances, and that the show would hopefully be back in the new year with a sponsor on board and with me and the producer back in the same jobs. But I knew that was a lie. They also still wanted us to produce the Christmas episode with a skeleton staff while the rest of the company was at the Christmas party in Ireland (where the head office was based). We did it out of professionalism.

Of course, after that I never heard from anyone at the company ever again, apart from when they emailed me my P45. The show returned a few months later with a new presenter and new producers. And that was it. No goodbyes, no thank yous for launching the show, and absolutely zero feedback.

At the time, I just tried to get on with my life. I was back to freelancing and needed to get work, especially as the job had been whisked away from me just as my wife and I were about to buy our first flat. It was only about a year later, when I was feeling down and started seeing a counsellor, that this job came up again during our sessions and I started to join the dots about just how much of an effect the whole episode had had on me.

I had suppressed my emotions immediately after the event, probably because they were too raw for me to even try to comprehend them, but had I allowed myself to feel them, I know there would have been a heady mix of guilt that I was crap enough to be released, resentment at how I had been treated, and disappointment at having lost a brilliant opportunity. The best job of my career …

Thankfully, a couple of years later, I landed an even better job doing similar stuff with a team of people who were amazing at all the things I needed from them and hadn't got at JOE: they were supportive, gave me plenty of feedback and were just lovely to be around.

BLANK

But that JOE dismissal hung over me for ages. And in many ways, it still does. That mix of lasting emotions is a kind of grief. Could I have done more to save my job? I'll never know. I felt so guilty for even being there in the first place. I clearly hadn't deserved the chance, and I had the five-month track record to prove it. Even though there were lots of things I made on that show that I had thought were really good, I was now doubting everything. As a presenter, I'd tried to take on as much responsibility as possible and as many challenges as I could. I had tried to improve where I could – and I thought I had – but any successes had been in spite of the powers that be at the company rather than with their help.

I realised I hadn't processed it all when I had a bit of a meltdown during a recording of my football podcast, which had been and still is a constant in my life, having been a weekly thing for a decade. My meltdown had nothing to do with the podcast but it was a trigger, and I had to email the guys afterwards and explain that I was not in a good place because of the whole JOE thing. They all instantly offered me more support than anyone at JOE ever had.

It's only been four years since this happened and I'm still not quite sure what I've learned from it. I think I may actually still be grieving it, to be honest. I've had some good things happen since then and some bad things, and I'm still here doing what I do, so it must have made me stronger. But I've had to block JOE. co.uk on all social media platforms, as whenever I see anything from them pop up, I get flashbacks to my dismissal, and those feelings of guilt and regret start to seep back in. I'm still grieving, and maybe I always will be.

But maybe that's a good thing, as it reminds me of how far I have come. I'm still here, I'm still in the game and, arguably, I'm doing better than ever. This episode didn't stop me or make me want to quit the business. It hurt me a lot, like a jab in the ribs, but I got up off the ropes and I'm still fighting.

GRIEF

I guess when you are grieving for a lost person or possession or relationship, most of the time there's nothing you can do about it, and maybe that was the case here. But that doesn't make it hurt any less. Life is full of lessons born out of pain, and grieving is a process that involves learning from those lessons and growing.

I still mention the job on my CV as I am proud of the show we created. JOE.co.uk has moved on to create some really excellent football content, though it is produced very differently now, but I take pride in the fact I was part of the team that started the process. I just wish it had ended differently.

And it isn't just the job itself you can mourn, but also the professional and personal relationships that may disappear if the job does. There was a very funny article on *The Onion* during the COVID-19 lockdown about two work friends who realise, once they are forced to work from home, that office banter was the only thing keeping them as friends. Outside the office, they have nothing in common. It's so common to miss that connection with co-workers, especially if it's the main thing that keeps you going through the day, even if outside of work it doesn't really exist. Our connections don't always have to be life-long, extra-strong bonds. They can simply be something that gets you through the nine-to-five.

Actor David Morrissey spoke about the grieving process of finishing an acting job and leaving behind the relationships you formed with the cast and crew. He said that, for him, it feels a bit like losing those people, especially as during the work process you build incredibly strong bonds with your colleagues – bonds that need to be strong to make the acting as believable as possible.

BLANK

David loves being in a cast of actors – it's like getting an immediate family each time he starts a job. Actors go through something so personal and raw at the same time on a project that it's impossible not to feel some sort of strong connection to each other. But David added that, after each job, most castmates move on to their next gig quickly, promising to stay in touch but often not managing it. From having breakfast, lunch and dinner with each other every day to no contact – that can feel like a loss every time.

But at least it's not just me that promises to stay in touch with ex-colleagues but never does. I've had many jobs, and made and lost plenty of work friends; and, like in that *Onion* article, some of them were just meant to be work friends and that's it, but it's still hard when you feel like you've invested time and effort in those people and that job, and that maybe it was all for nothing. But if the likes of David Morrissey and John Bradley are able to move on to the next thing and do it as brilliantly as they do, then maybe I can too. Maybe I can view each job and each work friendship as part of my journey. And maybe I can send a text to some of those past work colleagues a bit more often from now on.

———

There is also a sense of grief at losing a relationship, be it a romantic one or a working one. In the entertainment industry, a lot of writers make their name by collaborating with other people. David Baddiel did that, first with Rob Newman and later with Frank Skinner, but he spoke on our podcast about how the work led to the breakdown of both friendships. Baddiel and Newman famously had quite a big falling out and didn't speak to each other for a long time – until quite recently, in fact. David told us that while he was grateful for those collaborations, he now prefers not to have a central writing partner and to just work on his own stuff instead. He admitted that the strain of writing comedy – and collaborative partners not always being open to constructive criticism – can lead to tensions in the working relationship, and that, in turn, affects the friendship, which can be disappointing. Many people have lost good friends after falling out over work projects.

It was honestly refreshing hearing someone like David talk candidly about how those working relationships had been. He said that he felt he was the reasonable one most of the time, and he'd found that hard. When friendships blend into work collaborations or creative partnerships, the boundaries become blurred and it can make the nuts and bolts of writing comedy – or whatever it is you're working on – a lot harder. I had so much respect for David as a comedian before he came on the podcast, and that respect only increased after he spoke so openly about the strains put on these relationships. It made me realise that not only is it powerful to be vulnerable in front of other people, but that talking about the loss of friendships and working connections, especially amongst men, is rare and should be far more common, to normalise it.

David ended our conversation by saying he's been obsessed with trying to be himself on stage – wearily at times! – and it's only in the last eight or so years of doing solo shows that he's been able to do that. And, in a way, that comes from letting past working relationships go. That can be especially hard when those collaborations have been massively successful, as his with Newman and Skinner were, but sometimes it needs to be done so you can achieve true happiness and satisfaction in your working life.

Chapter 4:
Social Media

Not everyone is going to like you and that's fine. But I think there are so many people out there who don't understand that you aren't going to like everything. And that's fine. You don't have to then try and destroy that person because you didn't like them.

Carrie Hope Fletcher

Back in 2009, a friend on Facebook told me about this new social media platform they had discovered. It was very different to what we had become accustomed to with Facebook (and before that, the now-long-forgotten Myspace), as this platform only allowed users to post 140 characters, but according to my friend it was a lovely place, filled with lots of lively, positive, nuanced and interesting conversations and interactions – the perfect space to talk about interesting projects and interact with real-life celebrities. Even the mighty Stephen Fry had an account! So, I set about creating my profile and writing my first post …

For many, even the word 'Twitter' sends a shiver down their spine. For non-users, it's that place where everyone is mean to one another; for users it's … well, it's that place where everyone is mean to one another!

I seem to have had a very different experience on the platform, as I've always had a positive time. As a naturally introverted sort of person, social media has been a chance to connect with people from all walks of life, to interact and learn, and it has also given me the strength to clamber out of my shyness bunker in the real world.

The misconception of introverts is that we don't enjoy company. The truth is many of us love company, but situations in which we are forced to engage can sometimes lead to moments of intense anxiety. Social media gives us the power back – we can have social interactions at our own pace and (to a certain extent) on our own terms. For me, it has even allowed me to feel more comfortable in my real-life interactions.

By the year 2100, there will be in the region of 1.4 billion social media accounts of people who are deceased, and unless some sort of miracle cure for mortality has been discovered, I'll be one of those people.

In recent times, platforms like Facebook and Instagram have begun to pass 'legacy' accounts on to the family or friends of the deceased, to create memorial pages for their loved ones. A sort of online graveyard has developed, where folks can go and reminisce about happier times – and revisit images and past posts that are forever embedded into the platform. In fact, people can still leave messages to say how much they miss those they've lost, neatly compiled in the comments section. The rise in these memorialised accounts provides an opportunity to grieve online.

The huge growth in cybercrime has shone a spotlight on the need to protect the accounts of those who have passed on, and with deactivation often taking months to occur, and also requiring a death certificate in many cases, cybercriminals have started to take advantage by using such accounts to carry out financial scams.

For many going through bereavement, having an online memorial for a loved one can be a great comfort, and scheduled posts that are published posthumously have become a growing trend as those who know their time is limited start to plan their online legacy.

A website called FutureMe allows users to send themselves emails on scheduled dates, with one idea being that you can set yourself goals in life and see if they come true. However, many people are now using the service to speak to their loved ones from beyond the grave. Some may find this concept morbid or upsetting, but those who have experienced it have remarked on how comforting it has been as part of their healing process.

In 2010, blogger Esther Earl set up emails to be sent to her parents after her death from thyroid cancer. Her mum recalled receiving the first email: 'That letter made us weep, but also brought us great comfort – I think because of its intentionality, the fact that she was thinking about her future, the clarity with which she accepted who she was and who she hoped to become.'

Thinking about our online legacies is probably not a high priority for most of us, but more and more people have started to recognise that they will live on in the online world – and so they want to make sure they do so in the best possible way. Memorialised accounts on platforms like Facebook can be frozen – and although loved ones can visit them to reminisce, it doesn't allow for the profile to be changed or updated.

Things are improving, though, with specific people dubbed 'legacy contacts' being allowed access, like mediums in some sort of digital séance, but perhaps it's just another thing – along with wills, funeral arrangements and letters to the bank – that we have to consider as we head towards that inevitable moment.

———

I am fully aware that I might be in the minority when it comes to my positive experiences with social media, as over the last ten years, the optimism surrounding it has dwindled significantly.

Nearly every podcast episode we've done has at some point gone down the path of talking about the destructive and futile nature of social media – in particular Twitter, which always seems to be the most divisive platform – and we regularly discuss the lack of nuance we see there.

When we had Amanda Abbington on as a guest, she spoke about her experiences on Twitter. Amanda says she always wants to see more than one side of the conversation and likes to follow a broad range of people – and some of them she doesn't like or agree with, but she thinks it's sometimes good to know what those you might disagree with are saying. And because of this, people can make assumptions about Amanda and get extremely vehement about things, even when they have no idea about her politics or what she stands for – but like she says, getting into a fight on Twitter is often pointless.

The black-and-white nature of Twitter interactions that Amanda alluded to are never more present than when dealing with football fans. It's very much like being on the terraces, as Twitter has become a destination for angry supporters who want to vent about every aspect of every game.

Gary Lineker is certainly no stranger to being on the end of Twitter trolling. He told us that when he first joined Twitter, it wasn't so he could go and broadcast all his political opinions, but there have been a few times when he has gotten involved. The first was to do with football and FIFA and wanting to be hard on Sepp Blatter, because Gary felt that there was corruption – and he was eventually proved right. The second instance was when he expressed a degree of sympathy for refugees, for which he got attacked and even became front-page news in certain newspapers, something that really troubled Gary, as he found it hard to fathom why anyone would not feel compassion for families fleeing war-torn countries. And then the third issue was Brexit. Gary has never said which party he supports in elections, and there is a lot about politics that he has no interest in, but there are certain areas that he thinks are important and so has made the decision to air his views. And with Brexit, he really wondered what the hell we were doing … Gary knows a lot of people have disagreed with his stance, and he's recognised that and is fine with it, as he doesn't shy away from debate, but too often the dialogue just descends into abuse. And even though it's usually just a small number of people that are causing trouble, they shout the loudest, so we notice them more.

I hear this so often, both on the podcast and in conversations with friends and family – that, as a society, we have lost the notion of nuance. Or, to use a football metaphor, we are like two sets of supporters, each baying for the other's blood; we feel we have to be rivals, and that our own opinion is king. But much of what we discuss isn't binary, and life isn't black and white. For my part, I have doubled down on being more open and positive on platforms like Twitter, and injecting a bit of kindness back into social media feels like a duty of care for me. I have met some great people and found true friendships through social media; it's given me so much and I want to give a little back. Social media is an opportunity – one we often take for granted, as we are now so used to having it – and it's certainly allowed me to grow as a human being. I hope others will start to follow suit and spread a bit more love, and allow for more nuance in their interactions.

BLANK

———

Another aspect of social media that we hear a lot about is our innate desire for validation, and how the posts we put out there are fuel for this. Whether it's putting out info about a cause, saying something funny, being kind, arguing a point, calling someone out or just being plain abusive – these are all reliant on interactions or reactions, and they all stimulate us in some way.

There have been many times where I have taken a break from social media to have some time away from the noise, or because I'm feeling ignored, but it usually only lasts a day or two before I'm lured back in. There's a constant balancing act to using these platforms sensibly, and sometimes it's a struggle not to be on them 24/7.

Comedian and *Peep Show* star Isy Suttie gave us her own interpretation as to why we do this to ourselves. For her, social media and the internet play a significant role in our mental health. So often, we just pick up our phones without thinking about it, and this is our brain tricking us into thinking that Twitter or Facebook is our downtime. The reward system part of our brain is being stimulated by people liking our posts or interacting with us in a positive way, but then we might also get angry when we're online – and not necessarily because of people saying something to us directly, but just because there's something that we read that we disagree with. And so, actually, going on Twitter or checking our Facebook or Instagram feeds isn't really a break at all. It's not like putting on our favourite TV shows or doing something creative, like knitting or painting or cooking. Cutting back on social media is an area of her life that Isy told us she is continuing to work really hard on.

And maybe a bit of tough love is in order at times, when the energy we spend on social media is getting out of hand and we're starting to really feel the negative effects. One pod guest made the point that we are all in control of the amount we decide to use social media, and if it gets too much, then we need to address that. This guest often feels a little trapped because being online is such a big part of their job, and in those moments when they feel really low because of it, and they hear other people – for whom it isn't part of their job at all – struggling, they said they can't help thinking, 'If it's giving you shit, switch it off, delete it off your phone, get off it! What are you truly missing out on? Just switch the thing off, man!' In their view, if a person has the opportunity and the freedom to log off, then they should take advantage of that.

With the invention of social media, we've managed to create both the best and the worst thing for the human race. It's what simultaneously unites and divides us in equal measure.

It should have been different: this incredible, futuristic tool that allows us to communicate with anyone, anywhere in the world, at any time – opening up amazing opportunities to connect, to learn, to grow and to improve as individuals, as communities and as a species. But a decade later, and it's probably the one thing that will bring about the destruction of humanity.

It's such a human-being thing to take this incredible tool and completely ruin it. We have an uncanny ability to reduce the finest things in the world to rubble. Often literally. The problem is that, at our core, we are jealous, selfish beings, and it takes all our efforts to stop ourselves from just descending into massive green-eyed monsters who obsess over other people's successes. I remember first joining Twitter in 2009, and it was mostly Stephen Fry tweeting silly musings and people replying to them. That was basically it. And it was wonderful. I had a comedy song about Norwich City striker Grant Holt being called up to the England squad retweeted by Fry in 2012 and it was the highlight of my year. (Not Holt's, sadly – he didn't get the call-up, left Norwich not long after and has barely been seen since.)

But as Twitter grew, with more and more people joining each year, so did the clamour to be noticed – and, as ever, that led to people saying more and more ridiculous things at louder volumes. It's why people like Giles, who has a Twitter account that exudes positivity, are so important. Sadly, his approach appears to be pretty rare these days.

Even if you see yourself as a positive, friendly person, it's easy to get caught up in online arguments and say something stupid. The only way to really avoid any of that is just to delete your social media platforms. That's what comedian Ben Bailey Smith (aka Doc Brown) did a few years back, and he had a very compelling argument for his decision when he chatted with us.

He said that checking social media had become like a drug – getting that little hit of dopamine from the approval of strangers. He realised that working in the unreal world of show business meant he just wanted one area of his life that was real, and that meant not being online. Life now, he said, is like a fantasy; it's like those sci-fi movies of the 1980s where people are avatars and live in alternate realities. Ben's departure from social media wasn't a rejection of it, and he could still see the benefits of it, but he was mindful that, for some people, their social media 'persona' can bleed into their real life and that can become dangerous – especially if they lack self-awareness. He admitted that leaving social media had come at a cost work-wise, and he had missed out on jobs by not having a big following. But despite that, he felt it was a weight off his shoulders, and freed up a lot of time to be creative that he previously might have spent trying to get the perfect photo and curate his life online. His creative works – his books, his music and comedy, and his acting work – will be there long after he is gone, he added, and no one will care about his social media at that point anyway. He has returned to social media, but as a stripped-back version of his former online self.

In the podcast, you can hear me in the background while Ben is talking about this, saying to myself, 'I need to get off social media.' So much of what he said rang so true. It really has become a drug for some of us with addictive personalities. I find myself losing hours a day to scrolling, and not really even contributing – just scrolling, getting annoyed at other people's tweets, not replying and scrolling on. It isn't a very productive use of my time. I think I mainly go on in the first place to see if anyone has said anything about me and whether I need to respond, and to make sure I'm maintaining my public persona – which, let's face it, is a complete waste of time.

————

Susie Dent also wants to soak up other people's opinions, but not about herself and for different reasons. She admitted to us she is a very restless person and lives in her own head a lot of the time. She isn't particularly good at sitting down for hours and hours, and is much happier moving about, walking and distracting herself. Susie said that when she was at university studying languages, she was really scared of her own voice for a long time, so instead of trusting herself, she relied upon critics. She would go to the library and get out books and read about everyone else's opinions, and then try to make her own thoughts somehow fit in with their combined opinions. That lack of trust in her own opinion and her lack of self-conviction has stayed with her.

And I think I suffer from the same thing. I am often worried about saying the wrong thing and upsetting people, or being made an outcast for having outlandish opinions (not that many of my opinions are particularly outlandish, but there is always that worry you are going to say something stupid). It's particularly interesting to hear that someone like Susie – who I certainly look to as an expert who knows and works in facts – still struggles to trust in her own thoughts and beliefs. If someone as brilliant as her can't believe in herself, then what hope do the rest of us have?

Caring about what other people think is a very common trait that many, many people have to deal with. We are always told by super-successful Instagram influencers to just live our best lives and not compare ourselves to others or worry about what others think of us; that being oblivious to or ignoring how others see us is somehow freeing. I'm not sure I agree.

BLANK

I think actually this is an issue rooted in compassion. The minute we walked into Susie's house to record the podcast, she struck me as someone with bucketloads of compassion and kindness, and the two hours we spent in her company showed that to be absolutely true. What she let us know with that admission above, even if she didn't want to, was that compassion rules her every thought. She seemed to be so worried about showing compassion for those who don't quite hold similar views that she was happy to amend her thought process to accommodate them. And to me, that can be a really, really good thing. So often today we see people on TV and on social media resolutely stick to their terrible opinions – and sometimes their very offensive opinions, too. I'm not even sure half of them really believe what they're saying, but to be seen to be backtracking on your thoughts has somehow become a sign of weakness. Susie is showing us that it isn't. It's actually a sign of strength that you are able to listen to and care for people whose opinions you may not believe or even like, in an attempt to have a more rounded, worldly view.

If everyone, from all sides of the debate, did this a little bit more often, I think we'd have a much kinder – and probably better functioning – society.

Chapter 5:
Sleep

When you sleep, your brain washes away many of the toxins so if you are missing out on sleep, you are literally poisoning your brain.

Fiona Murden

Being a twenty-something trying to make it in a rock band,
I viewed sleep as just another thing that seemed to get in
the way. It was low on my list of priorities, and so all the time
it wasn't noticeably detrimental to my heath or well-being,
I seemed to live by the rule (to quote Warren Zevon) 'I'll sleep
when I'm dead'.

My first major brush with sleep deprivation began on Friday,
23 June 2000, at about 7 a.m. I was busily setting up a two-
person tent in the field adjacent to the New Bands Tent at
Glastonbury Festival. The band I was in at the time, Little 10,
were playing there the following morning, and we wanted to
set up camp as close as possible – but also forgo any VIP areas
and be among the regular punters, so we could soak up the true
atmosphere of a festival that, truth be told, we never thought
we'd ever actually perform at!

The thought that was throbbing intensely in my head while I
grappled with the unwieldy tent poles was that a good night's
sleep was imperative for me to be able to perform at my best
the following day. As I danced around, flailing with the ground
sheet, a panic ensued that I had not experienced before. Being
in a band often meant late nights and unsettled sleep – our
transit van being our usual base for the night – so why was
this moment any different? Perhaps it was the size of the event
ahead of us, or the fact that I hadn't slept in the last 24 hours as
we'd travelled through the night in a rather small car, or maybe
it was just that I'd reached that point where my body was telling
me enough was enough.

In truth, it was all these things, and the combination of realising
how important it was to sleep and the lack of sleep I'd already
experienced caused me to have an attack of anxiety. I tried to
make light of it at the time, and I'm pretty sure no one else that

was with me realised I was potentially crashing while we were in the midst of our greatest achievement.

Suffice to say, that night I did manage a few hours, and the next day, when we were waiting at the side of the stage, I was feeling a lot more relaxed and had managed to shake off what I'd experienced the previous day. But as time passed and I experienced other moments of sleep anxiety, my relationship with sleep became a fractured one. We were like a couple going through a trial separation, trying desperately to see if we could make things work going forward.

I started to brush off my lack of sleep as just being my 'thing', and 'burning the candle at both ends' was my go-to phrase when describing my habits. I even started to revel in the fact I could still function (albeit not always very well) on very little sleep. Sleep was for wimps, and when you're a rock and roller, it just gets in the way.

Before I knew it, sleep and I had started divorce proceedings.

THE CURLY-HEADED KID IN THE THIRD ROW

In 1959, at the age of 32, Radio DJ Peter Tripp, nicknamed 'The Curly-headed Kid in the Third Row', decided to embark on a seemingly impossible and also somewhat ludicrous experiment.

What lay ahead of him was far removed from the everyday patter of a 1950s DJ. Though he was known for his strait-laced approach, Tripp had a dark side to him. He was a risk-taker, an edgy cigarettes-for-breakfast kinda guy, who was determined not to let his peers in the industry outdo him. The task he was about to undertake was just the sort of thing to put him on the map – but it would also lead him to a desperate dark place, on the brink of psychosis.

The stunt, known as a 'wake-a-thon', would see the DJ attempt to stay awake for some two hundred hours. The consequences of this were rapid and devastating. At first, Tripp appeared relaxed and confident, broadcasting in his usual way, but within the first 24 hours, things start to spiral, with his off-air antics in particular starting to cause concern. Knowing this would prove to be valuable research, sleep experts were brought in to sit with Tripp and take notes on his every move, mood and manner, and the station also supplied him with stimulants to keep the stunt going.

One hundred hours in, Tripp began to hallucinate: he thought his shoes were filled with spiders, that a chest of drawers was on fire, and he saw mice running around. These were conscious dreams caused by the brain's need for REM sleep – when deprived of it, the brain will go into REM cycles while the person is awake, making the person see things. Nearing the end of his two hundredth hour, Tripp had started to see a friend's face in a clock, and had even started to wonder if he was himself Peter Tripp or the friend. Ever the professional, most of Tripp's paranoia and delusions surfaced off-air, and somehow he was able to pull himself together while broadcasting his regular show.

When the stunt was over, Tripp slept for a solid 13 hours and appeared to recover fairly quickly, but not long after, he was implicated in a financial scandal and lost his job and marriage. Tripp and several other DJs had been playing particular records on their shows in return for gifts, and as he had been accepting these bribes prior to the wake-a-thon, some people wondered whether his visceral paranoia during the stunt was a reflection of guilt about his wrongdoing behind the scenes.

His subsequent downfall was rapid and the psychological damage continued for a long time after his sleepless marathon, with Tripp even thinking he was an imposter of himself. The lasting effects of his period of sleep deprivation show just how essential sleep is in our lives. With no sleep at all, we will die; if we go without it for a period of time, it can cause a form of psychosis, as it did for Peter Tripp; and even a night or two of bad sleep in a week can cause us mental and physical problems.

And 'catching up' on lost sleep is no simple matter. The sleep specialist Matthew Walker has said: 'You're trying to sleep off a debt that you've lumbered your brain and body with during the week, and wouldn't it be lovely if sleep worked like that? Sadly, it doesn't. Sleep is not like the bank, so you can't accumulate a debt and then try and pay it off at a later point in time.'

I think we would all do well to remember that.

———

As I describe how my relationship with sleep became so fractured in my twenties, it sounds like it was a choice, but in truth my environment, circumstances and state of mind at the time were to blame. Unsocial hours, creating and performance were at the heart of my sleeping problems, but at the time, I wasn't self-aware enough to realise that insomnia might also be an issue.

One of the first times the subject of sleep came up on the podcast was when we spoke to actress Rebecca Callard. I'd known Rebecca was an insomniac, and was keen to share notes with her.

Rebecca's experiences with disturbed sleep happen most nights, and because of that she has learned to cope with it, but sometimes she'll have a particularly bad run of it and she'll be at the end of her tether. When that happens, she said, it's as if her brain and body can't take any more, and if she is somehow – or in her words, 'mercifully' – given one night of sleep, that one night can be enough to rejuvenate her.

She told us her insomnia began to get really bad when she was pregnant with her son Sonny, and when she talked to her mum about it, she discovered that she'd been a bad sleeper as a child too. She'd always found it very difficult to go to sleep, and would close her eyes and see strange things – almost hallucinations.

Like Rebecca, when children came into my life, the full force of my own insomnia came to the fore, and those lost hours really started to take a toll on my physical and mental well-being, with heightened anxiety and periods of ill health I can attribute solely to sleep deprivation.

Like with many of the subjects addressed in this book, being able to listen and talk to others in a similar situation has been a huge source of comfort, and has given me a chance to look at my own strategies and find ways to improve. With sleeping, it has been about not getting het up and anxious when sleep doesn't come easily, and something Dawn French said when she was on the podcast really struck home.

Dawn said that, when she can't sleep, she gets up and has a cup of tea and a bit of toast, and literally acts as if it's early evening again. And somehow, after an hour or so, her brain starts to go, 'I think I'm a little bit tired again.' Then she can go to sleep. It's like replaying the end of the evening, as if you somehow didn't do it right the first time – like maybe you didn't go through the stages correctly.

That was a massive help for me, and it's something I try on those nights when sleep and I aren't seeing eye to eye. Like all relationships, we're continuing to work on it – and I'm hoping that, over time, sleep and I will be in a place where we can discuss renewing our vows.

We each have our own relationship with sleep. Some people are proud to say they don't sleep – mainly business-y people, who like to boast about only sleeping four hours a night so they have more time to do business-y things. Donald Trump famously only sleeps a few hours a night and he managed to work his way to the White House, although I suspect many of his waking hours are spent getting into Twitter feuds, not doing any actual work, and generally being the worst human alive. Some people can only function if they get a lot of sleep. Some people sleep during the day and work at night. And some people – well, they don't sleep at all, and not by choice.

Creative people in particular seem to suffer from insomnia, and when David Baddiel joined us on the podcast, he spoke about it as something that, by now, is just a part of him. Like a leg or an arm. David repeated a quote from Bertrand Russell – 'Men who are unhappy, like men who sleep badly, are always proud of the fact' – and said that he thinks that being an insomniac is one of those negative hallmarks that you have to live with. He's been an insomniac for so long he can't think of himself any other way.

It's probably a similar story for a lot of insomniacs, but David tries his best not to see it as an affliction and instead turns it into a positive. So, on nights when he's really struggling with sleep, he will tap into his creativity and jot down random ideas. They might not become anything, but many do. It's a different story on tour, however, and he's had many sleepless nights before shows, worrying that because he'll be so tired, he's going to be shit the next night. Thankfully, Doctor Theatre – which actors talk about as the cure when performers feel terrible before a show but somehow make a miraculous recovery on stage, and then feel awful again afterwards – nearly always sorts things out.

David turning something that is really quite shit (let's be honest) into a positive is inspiring. I'm not an insomniac, but sleeplessness can still affect any of us. I've had loads of nights where I can't get to sleep because my mind is working on some crazy creative idea, or I wake up in the middle of the night because of a lightbulb moment.

During 2013, I was writing comedy football songs for an animated YouTube series called *The Football Special*, and because I was having to write a song a week and deliver them in monthly batches, I was *always* writing. It meant that I was constantly having to sing little riffs and hooks into my phone recorder app, and on lots of occasions I would wake up in the middle of the night with a tune in my head and, barely conscious, sing it into my phone and hope by the morning it made sense. Thankfully, a few of them did and became fully-fledged songs a few weeks later.

BLANK

I used to be one of those people who prided themselves on sleeping well, for long periods, and being able to do it quite literally anywhere. On the sofa in front of a movie? Of course. Planes? No problem. Long bus rides? Just give me a pillow and I'm down. I once slept under a bush outside a friend's house because he locked us out after a party, and I hadn't even been drinking.

Then I became someone who not only slept a lot, but needed that sleep. If I didn't get a decent seven or eight hours a night, I would get very cranky and the next day would be a write-off. I would moan incessantly at work about not having slept enough, completely unaware that in the office there would probably be – taking into account the national average – a good handful of people who hadn't slept the night before, or who'd slept terribly.

But weirdly, since starting the podcast, where the theme of sleep comes up fairly regularly, I have started to struggle with sleep. The arrival of my daughter has obviously been an influential factor too. There was one point in the first few weeks after she came home from the hospital that I woke up at the kitchen sink at 3 a.m. with absolutely no idea why I was there. (More on parenting later in the book.)

We had one guest come on the podcast the day after a particularly stressful sleepless night. They had been up late writing for the second series of a very successful show, only to lose the episode they were working on after their computer crashed. They'd spent the entire night trying to get it back and jot down the bits they could remember, and then they had to come and see us the following morning to chat about blank moments, having just had one big blank moment all night. In hindsight, they could have easily cancelled and we would have totally understood, but it shows what sort of person they were that they kept the engagement.

What resulted, though, was a really intense hour-long chat, and we could see first-hand what happens when someone has zero sleep. Something in their filter had been switched off, and this guest just talked and talked about everything that had been troubling them in their career and their life. It was like an honesty switch had been turned on. They might have been like that on a regular day, too – I don't know, as I'd never met them before – but it ended up being one of the most candid episodes we've ever done.

It did make me wonder, afterwards, what a lack of sleep does to the brain. It clearly isn't good. Giles has already talked about Peter Tripp's wake-a-thon – a lack of sleep clearly had a profound effect on the DJ's mental state and his actions. It's why we see so many road signs encouraging people not to drive if they haven't slept.

Our sleep-deprived guest on the podcast admitted they had written a lot that night in an attempt to claw back the episode they had lost – and that, actually, a lot of it was potentially better than what they'd written in the first place. This can sometimes be the case with rewrites, but they aren't usually forced on you so dramatically.

While researching this book, we went back through every episode to see what we could learn from each of our guests' stories, and this one intrigued me the most. So I decided to try a little experiment of my own: I would try writing my parts of the book late at night, on as little sleep as possible. Would I end up writing much better stuff as a result? Would the lack of sleep open up some part of my brain I hadn't previously explored? Would I wake up the next morning, head on my laptop keys, with thousands upon thousands of words that were gold – or maybe just the letter 'z' repeated hundreds of times because of how I'd slept on it?

The answer was none of the above. I barely made it past midnight, and when I did manage to stay awake, not a lot of writing happened. Then I would try to sleep and get annoyed at myself for not being able to, like I'd somehow failed as a human being. Intentionally not sleeping is one thing; staying awake when you are trying to sleep is another. Those times I want to sleep but can't, I always seem to get overcome by thoughts of failure, like I can't even do this one thing that I need to do at this exact moment. I literally have one job and I can't even do that! Then you start to resent yourself and get annoyed, which only makes getting to sleep even harder.

But listening to the experience of our sleep-deprived guest and then trying my own sleep experiment (and failing) has left me with a greater understanding and appreciation of the role sleep plays in people's lives and creativity. Some need it, some don't need it, some need it and can't get it, and some don't need it and get a lot of it. It's certainly made me more aware that the next time I moan to others about not getting enough sleep, I should try to be more considerate and aware of who I might

be moaning to and what they might be going through. Especially
people who used to get a decent night's sleep and now don't –
for example, new parents. Since starting the podcast, my wife
and I had our first child, and as she grew bigger and our nights
became shorter and shorter, I really began to relate to people
who have sleep problems.

———

When she joined us on the podcast, Isy Suttie talked about not
sleeping and how it affects her performing. She admitted she
used to write off people who complained about not getting any
sleep with little ones, because her first child slept like a dream.
But her second was a different story. Sleeping improved with
a night nanny, but when both children got chicken pox, there
were times when Isy and her husband Elis would spend all night
swapping bedrooms to look after each of them, like ships passing
in the night. At one point, she fell asleep while reading a bedtime
story to her five-year-old, who was in so much pain that she'd
only stop crying if she had a story read to her. By this stage, Isy
and Elis were begging their children to let them have just a little
bit of sleep, especially as any writing or performing work the
next day would have to be done on zero sleep.

Thankfully – this conversation took place just before our baby
arrived, and I was no doubt looking very worried across the
table as she spoke – Isy said that sleep matters did improve.
I think the idea that things get better is a good coping
mechanism, not just for when you're losing sleep, but for life in
general. Most things are a phase – good or bad – and knowing
there's an end to them can be a helpful way of dealing with the
shit when it's happening.

Isy also recounted a story about how work anxiety led to a lack
of sleep. She was performing in a play called *Frog in Love*, about
a frog that falls in love with a duck, which I'm gutted I never

got to see. Because the cast had taken a break from performing before being back in rehearsals ahead of taking the show to the Edinburgh Fringe, and because she had to do a range of accents (she was playing the duck, who was Scouse, as well as a Cockney rat and various other roles), Isy was so worried about being rusty or putting in a subpar performance that she couldn't sleep. It led to some pretty serious bouts of insomnia.

Then she told us about a time when struggling to sleep had a direct, and very painful, effect. While she was working on the Channel 4 series *Shameless*, Isy spent her nights in a hotel in Manchester lying awake and worrying about being so tired she'd forget her lines in the morning. This went on for three nights, and by the third, she was so sleep-deprived that she was desperate to catch any bit of sleep she could. Before the minibus arrived the next morning to take her to set, she stayed in bed as long as she could, hoping for a few minutes' sleep. But when she raced to have a super-quick shower, because the room was blacked out to try to help her doze off, she didn't see the open bathroom door and smashed into it face first.

Of course, everyone in the minibus noticed the massive black eye that was developing, and once they reached the set, she was sent to A&E. The doctors advised her to take a few days off, but the director said, 'No way,' so she went straight back to set and they just slapped some make-up on her black eye and got filming.

If that isn't an advert for a decent night's sleep, I don't know what is – and I now want to go back to that episode to see if I notice Isy's black eye. Most of the time, lack of sleep just makes you slow and lethargic, but Isy's story is a warning that it can physically hurt you, too. In fact, there are scientific reasons why you should get a decent night's sleep, and why not having one can not just lead to blank moments, but also damage your brain.

———

We all know that feeling when you haven't slept well for a while: it's like you're functioning at half-speed, and even basic tasks become incredibly difficult. It feels like your brain isn't working properly – and that's because it isn't, really. We spoke to psychologist Fiona Murden on an episode to try to find out the science behind blank moments, and she had some pretty eye-opening explanations for what happens when you have one of those nights where your eyes are open too much.

What she told us was that, when you are tired, your brain starts to work differently. For example, the frontal lobe, which is the bit of your brain that controls your logical responses, gets taken over by your emotions, and that's why you fly off the handle at the smallest things when you are tired. And it gets worse. A 2015 study by Dr Maiken Nedergaard at the University of Rochester Medical Center found that, when we are asleep, our brains are clearing themselves of neurological toxins. When you don't sleep, that can't happen, so you are literally poisoning your brain.*

And with sleep, there is a natural cycle which experiments have shown to last about four hours. Historically, Fiona said, people would wake up after four hours, do something mundane for an hour like pray, read or talk with a neighbour, and then go back to sleep. Of course, these days if you wake in the middle of the night, most people will fight it and try to get back to sleep immediately. It begs the question of where the now-ubiquitous eight-hour sleeping pattern came from.

This natural cycle might help to explain why so many creative people have ideas in the middle of the night or when they are just about to drop off. Isy Suttie asked us that very thing – whether we ever have an idea for something creative just before

SLEEP

---

* https://www.urmc.rochester.edu/news/story/4254/study-that-shows-how-brain-cleans-itself-while-we-sleep-honored-by-aaas.aspx

we're about to go to sleep, and what we do. And David Baddiel also mentioned it. Both of them said they like to write down an idea when it comes to them at night, and then revisit it in the morning. After learning more about how our brains work, these night-time creative moments and a lot of creative people's links to insomnia are starting to make sense.

In fact, these truth bombs from Fiona had a profound effect on me after recording the pod. I suddenly understood why I don't feel like a complete person after a bad night's (or multiple nights') sleep. And actually, I think we can use this information to let ourselves off the hook a little bit. Those sleepless nights aren't really your fault, and you need to be kind to yourself, give yourself some time to recover, and accept the fact that the next day is probably a write-off.

It's like getting in a car that's low on fuel. You wouldn't blame the car for running on empty, you'd go to a petrol station and fill it up – and that's what we should be doing for our bodies and our brains.

With all this in mind, here are the *Blank Podcast*'s top ten tips for a better night's sleep:

1. Learning to quiet your mind can be a helpful skill, both for navigating stressful daytime periods and for falling asleep at night.

2. Steer clear of stressful activities before bed. (Don't watch *Question Time*.)

3. Put your to-do list down on paper.

4. If you do wake up, get up and try rebooting your bedtime routine.

5. Try the Wim Hof breathing tutorial, available on YouTube.

6. Try to exercise each day.

7. Turn your phone off at least an hour before bed.

8. Read a few pages from a book just before you go to sleep.

9. No caffeine after 5 p.m., and avoid heavy alcohol consumption.

10. Try a melatonin supplement, and/or magnesium.

Alternatively, you could go one step further and take the sage advice of Isy Suttie's mum …

Isy's mum cannot to go to sleep unless she's read a couple of pages of a book before bed, as she finds that it clears her mind. It's something I've taken to doing in recent years myself, and so Isy asked what kinds of things I read. She said her mum recommended reading really boring stuff as anything too exciting doesn't work – in fact, she even reads manuals before bed, so perhaps the how-to-descale-the-coffee-machine instructions might be a good call?

Whatever works for you!

Chapter 6:
Social Anxiety

My blank moments are when I'm in rooms with people I don't know and how awkward I feel sometimes. I've gone to things at the BBC and not been able to open my mouth and I've gone home without speaking a word to anybody, just out of complete crippled shyness.

Reece Shearsmith

Social anxiety is very common, and we have all had moments when we've felt anxious in a crowd or on edge at a social gathering. But when this anxiety becomes more frequent or incapacitating, our social lives can become a bit overwhelming.

It is often hard to imagine that people whose job it is to perform would ever suffer from social anxiety. But they do. The Oscar-winning actress Kim Basinger once said of her own experiences of anxiety: 'When I came to Hollywood, I could wear a bikini, but I was in misery because people were looking at me. So I wore baggy clothes and watched other girls get the big parts and awards. I used to go home and play piano and scream at night to let out my frustrations. And this led to my agoraphobia.'

How social anxiety develops and what triggers it varies wildly from person to person. From my own experiences of it, I know that I'm at my most anxious in larger groups or when speaking to a larger audience, which I have to do during author events. It is, of course, totally natural to feel nervous, and for me the best antidote is often intense preparation – what I'm going to say or do needs to be very well thought out in my head, otherwise the temptation to bolt from the room can be quite overwhelming.

I've learned and implemented my own strategies for these times – with varying degrees of success – and my own experiences with blank moments nearly always spawn from incidents of social anxiety.

The first time we discussed the subject on the podcast was with actor and writer Reece Shearsmith, who spoke candidly about his experiences. His blank moments happen when he is in a room with people he doesn't know, because of how awkward it makes him feel. He told us about times he's gone to BBC events and not been able to open his mouth out of complete fear – he wasn't able to see an 'in' with anybody, and when you don't know anyone, it can be so difficult to march up to someone and say hello. Reece said there have been times he's looked around for someone he might know, and if he can't see anyone, he turns around and goes home without speaking a word to another person. He's crippled with shyness, to the point where he actively avoids those kind of situations now, and if he does have to go to events, he often just stands and listens and doesn't participate in conversations, for fear of people thinking he's boring or uninteresting.

As a child, I was painfully shy in social situations, and it was an awkwardness that continued to haunt me throughout my teenage years. I attempted to fight it off by acting up in class, and multiple school reports described me as disruptive. I perversely thought that by seeking attention, I would overcome my lack of desire for it. (It didn't make sense then, and it makes even less sense now as I recall it.) Trying to combat introversion with over-the-top extroversion was my default, but it only led to short periods of respite from my feelings of inadequacy and being out of place.

Like a car running out of fuel, my later teenage years saw me withdraw more and interact less with my peers, sticking to more comfortable one-on-one scenarios and constantly overanalysing pretty much everything I said – a trait I've never been able to shake. This is something we chatted about with presenter Emily Dean on the *Blank Podcast* – the way we sometimes behave like we're sports pundits doing a post-match analysis of our own conversations.

Emily mentioned that she was reading something about how unnatural it is to hear or watch ourselves, and this is to do with the brain and how we are essentially primed to watch out for enemies. We tend to perceive things and process information in a negative light because we are looking to confirm our own worst fears, like 'that predator is going to eat me'. And oddly, that happens when we see or hear ourselves, too, and so there are times for all of us when we are our own worst Twitter troll.

This kind of post-match analysis sparks discomfort in any future encounters. Evaluating our conversations negatively is a prime symptom of social anxiety, but not an obvious one.

––––––

Doing the podcast has been both a blessing and a curse for my own social neuroses, and my desire to get out there and conquer my shyness has led me to a more comfortable place. Meeting and talking not only to people I've never met before, but also to people I greatly admire and am inspired by, is one hell of a kick in the teeth to the shyness demon. However, my anxiety often gets a second wind, and that little worm in my ear begins to nag at me: 'Why did you say that?' and 'You shouldn't have said that', and so on and so on.

To get a greater understanding of what social anxiety really is, we had a Q&A with psychologist and friend of the podcast Fiona Murden to give us a bit of insight …

1. **What is social anxiety?**
    It's a form of anxiety disorder that comes about in normal, everyday social situations. It's an ongoing fear of being judged by others and a discomfort at the idea of being watched, with an associated concern of being humiliated or embarrassed. It's often linked to low self-esteem and depression. It can be related to one particular type of situation, such as work meetings or presentations, and often people will worry for days, weeks or even months before a specific event. Or it can be more general, relating to a whole range of social circumstances. It can interfere with work, school and being socially active.

2. **Is there a difference between being an introvert and having social anxiety?**

Yes, most definitely. Introversion is about where someone gets their energy from. An introvert needs time alone to recharge, but that doesn't mean they are anxious about social situations; it's simply that they need time away from others to give them mental space. Introverts may be extremely socially confident and gregarious.

3. **Are there any basic strategies we can try to help us overcome socially anxious moments?**

You can talk kindly and positively to yourself in your head – really watch your self-talk and try to push it towards kind rather than harsh. Focus on other people, not yourself. We tend to focus so much on whether people are looking at or judging us, and it's really helpful to watch and think about other people instead. Really listen to what other people are saying, rather than concentrating on what you're going to say next, for example. Think through how the other person is feeling. Try really hard to listen and genuinely connect – and remember that people forgive a lot (and are less likely to judge you) if you give them the time to talk and feel listened to. Remind yourself that even if you feel anxious, fearful or worried, other people are unlikely to notice. Most people are too worried about themselves and what they think others are thinking of them. Lastly, look after the physical factors that induce anxiety: reduce caffeine intake; if you're drinking alcohol, do it in moderation; be physically active; and try to get enough sleep.

4. **Has the advent of social media increased social anxiety?**

It's complicated. Social media has increased levels of anxiety in general, which may then increase people's propensity for social anxiety in real-life situations. People with social anxiety tend to prefer online social interactions, however – though research suggests that despite being perceived as helpful, it tends to result in poorer overall levels of well-being.

5. **What advice would you give to someone experiencing social anxiety for the first time?**
   Be gentle with yourself and be kind – it's okay, a lot of people feel this way. Talk to someone you trust. Try mindfulness apps like Headspace, and if it becomes a persistent problem, seek professional help – I would suggest acceptance and commitment therapy or cognitive behavioural therapy as helpful treatments.

For me, one of the great benefits of doing a podcast is that each of the conversations is recorded in its entirety – and listening back to episodes for this book has allowed me to address my own paranoia about how I interact with others, as I'm able to conduct a sort of forensic examination. As is often the way, there's a stark difference between reality and the perception in my head, and my overwhelming desire to make a good impression – which feels so intense in the moment – often sounds diluted when I hear the conversation later.

As much as it is easy to crucify yourself over interactions with others because you want to make the best impression, it's also important to remember that, as long as you are yourself and you remain authentic, then most of the time, people really don't give a shit. This isn't a popularity contest, we aren't pitching on *Dragons' Den* or performing on *X Factor*. We have to treat each conversation as a chance to learn and evolve – and that is one of the biggest reasons why I wanted to start this podcast. I want to learn and grow as a person, and I feel I can only really do that through social interaction; and so, for the time being, any anxieties I have are kept (as much as possible) at arm's length.

Eleanor Roosevelt once said, 'You gain strength, courage, and confidence by every experience in which you really stop to look

BLANK

fear in the face. You are able to say to yourself, "I have lived through this horror. I can take the next thing that comes along."' The *Blank Podcast* is my training, and slowly but surely, my confidence muscles are growing, with each episode another kilo of courage added to the dumb-bells of change.

JIM

I am a total fake when it comes to social engagements. I have somehow managed to curate the image of a friendly, engaging, fun person who is great at parties and revels in the attention, but 99 times out of 100 I would much rather be at home watching a box set than at any social gathering. I can't even begin to count the number of times I've been on my way to some sort of social event – whether it's a party at a bar or dinner at a restaurant, or something fancier like an awards ceremony – and wanted to turn the car around and go straight home before I've even got there. Wherever I go out, I feel anxious.

Even when I get invited to very small dinner parties with close friends, I still feel on edge, as if I am expected to perform or act a certain way. There's absolutely no way that I can just sit quietly in the corner, listening to conversations and minding my own business. I'm way too far gone for that now. People would assume something was up with me, rather than believing I might just prefer being quiet and not talking. Contrary to the image I have built of myself, and what people seem to think of me, I *like* being quiet. But even among friends, I struggle to do that. I'm expected to perform and be funny and entertaining, and so that's what I'm going to do – even if I don't want to.

And then there are the parties where there are new people. I have a chance to create a new persona every time, but I always go for the same one: the nice, funny, chatty guy. I find introducing myself to new people incredibly tiring and boring, and I feel like, because I don't have a normal job, I have to justify what I do. 'Oh, the money isn't great, but I enjoy it.' (I don't always.) 'I get to work from home a lot, which is great.' (It isn't.) 'The freedom is a blessing.' (It's often the exact opposite.)

When I was younger, I would drink to get through these sorts of engagements, but after many, many incidents – some of which ended with me in hospital – my drinking days are behind me. So I have to grit my teeth and get through it, and deal with my self-doubt. What if they don't like me? What if they think I'm an idiot? What if they move on to another conversation? As I'm talking, usually at a hundred miles an hour, I am analysing their faces for clues as to whether they are enjoying my company or not. If their eyes dart to something that isn't me – someone behind me or something else in the room – I start panicking. And I also panic if they don't follow my anecdote with one of their own, or they don't say something to continue the conversation. But the truth is that sometimes you talk to people and you just aren't going to have a decent conservation with them. It happens.

But my anxiety at parties – and this is true for many people, I suspect – comes down to an overwhelming desire to be liked. Loved, even. It's probably why I do stand-up comedy. In fact, I am far more comfortable standing on stage telling jokes to an audience of 200 than I am at a party with a handful of people. Knowing they are all paying attention to me and (mostly) enjoying what I am saying is far, far less anxiety-inducing than trying to hold a one-on-one conversation with someone who isn't that interested.

Interestingly, and somewhat pleasingly, comedian Rachel Parris agrees. She admitted she went through a period of intense anxiety where she couldn't leave the house to do anything, but when she did finally do a gig, she was actually relieved to discover she was fine. Well, on stage. Everything around the experience of gigging was a nightmare; from the travel to get there, to preparing her set, to practising the words, and she arrived at the venue shaking, but when she got on stage, everything felt okay. That was a relief, she said, because she realised she could still do the thing she was good at, even if her brain was trying to stop her getting there. It was a moment's peace in a time of real anxiety.

———

This desire to be liked is something that affects all of us in one way or another. (If it doesn't, you may be a sociopath and might want to get that checked out.) Whether we want to be liked for our company and chat, like I do, or for our business skills, practical skills, organisational skills or whatever else, we all want to be appreciated by others. It's part of what makes us human – that desire to be appreciated and to connect with other people.

And while what I've said probably paints me as a desperately needy person who cares way too much about what people think, I don't necessarily think it's a bad thing (although I have had that viewpoint challenged, both on the podcast and later in this book). This isn't a conclusion I have come to easily, but it is one I have reached since starting the podcast. And a major factor in reaching it was when we were recording episode four, and Susie Dent was talking about her lack of conviction in her beliefs (which we touched on in Chapter Four).

She went on to tell a story about an instance in which she chose to adapt her opinions. She had been writing a newspaper column on language, and the subject was the 'x' that members and supporters of the LGBTQ+ community have added to the word 'women' to be inclusive of trans women and non-binary individuals. Susie, as a lexicographer, was struggling to get her head around it, because 'womxn' is almost unpronounceable, but she ended her article by suggesting that if the 'x' had made her rethink everything connected to this word, then it was doing its job.

I remember saying to her afterwards that, in my view, being considerate of other people's views and thoughts wasn't a bad thing. Caring about what people think, whether it is about the things they are passionate about or what they think about you, is a *good* thing. It shows you are compassionate and are connected to others. But that isn't to say it's always a bad thing to try to free yourself of others' opinions about you, and yes, I do appreciate that might be coming across as contradictory. Not caring what others think about you can be liberating – and healthy, too. But there's a balance to be struck. Caring too much what other people think can be tiring, like a weight holding you down, but not caring at all can leave you feeling disconnected.

BLANK

When we chatted with a guest who is a female TV presenter, she talked about trying to live life not caring too much what other people think. Or at least other people whose opinions don't matter. She admitted that she gives very few fucks about the opinions of others, which is why positive and negative reviews of her work do not affect her as much as they might other people. If a TV show she is working on does well, then that's great, she's happy; but if it doesn't, she doesn't wallow in self-pity, she simply tries to work on making it better next time. Comments from viewers, especially negative ones, merely roll off her like water off a duck's back. And she pays little attention to online engagement, because – for her and many other women working in TV – engagement doesn't always mean nice comments, to say the least.

I find it very hard not to care what people think about me in all areas of life, but particularly work, especially as so much of your perceived success in the entertainment industry is based on likeability. When I'm on stage, I want people to like me and I believe there are very few comedians who don't feel the same way. Only a few are able to pull off being curmudgeonly and make it funny. I've been told by promoters that I am likeable on stage and that this is one of my strengths as a performer. This is lovely, but it does mean I now rely on audiences liking me, which puts on a fair amount of pressure. But it isn't just within comedy that I need people to like me; if I am doing a casting, I want the casting director to like me; if I am pitching for work, I want the commissioning editor to like me. It's neverending.

Putting yourself out there to be liked, or judged, is unavoidable at times. And it's true that when we open ourselves up to comments and engagement – not just with work things, but in life in general – we don't always get back what we were looking for. This guest's approach to not caring what other people think was refreshing, and it actually stopped me in my tracks a bit during the podcast and made me reconsider my own approach.

I had just relayed a story on this episode about the time I worked with a friend who was doing some life coaching. She'd attempted to help me get some clarity on everything I was trying to do in life. Mainly work stuff, but also personal stuff. One of the exercises she got me to do was to ask three of my closest friends to describe me however they saw fit. So I asked Andy, Callum and Rob, the groomsmen at my wedding and three guys I've known for a combined total for 64 years. They know me very, very well. I've been sick in Rob's house numerous times; I consoled Andy after he was attacked at a bar; I walked the Scottish Highlands with Callum and got very lost. They all came back with lovely things, to be honest, but the one word they all used was 'resilient'. Like I said in the chapter on imposter syndrome, if some people all use the same word to describe you, then you must possess that quality. If you hold those people in high regard and believe their words to be true, then that must surely be fact. Even if you don't believe it yourself.

I was pretty confident in this approach, but our guest wasn't so sure about the need to get approval from other people, and it did make me think about why I'd needed that. And it made me think about how different our experiences were. As a straight white man – the most boring of all versions of human being – the only person pushing me down is me. But anyone who is not a straight white man automatically has a lot of straight white men pushing them down before they even begin to think about doing it to themselves. So it made sense that this guest, a female TV presenter, had a different experience of this kind of thing, and that when I told her about this exercise, she wasn't so sure. She asked why I should care what anyone else thinks, and reckoned I should ask *myself* if I think I'm resilient. She told me my opinion was the only one that matters when it comes to me.

Even after all my soul-searching about why I want to be liked and what people think of me, my social anxiety remains – and it may do forever. It's not something you just get rid of, but it can be worked around and worked on.

––––––

When Rachel Parris was a guest on the *Blank Podcast*, she quickly got on to the subject of social anxiety, and she admitted to struggling with it a lot in her work as a comedian.

She admitted she gets anxious before shows, despite how experienced she is with them now. She is a very different person before and after a show. She worries she can come off as not very warm before a show, because inside she is very anxious and worrying about it. A lot of it comes down to what kind of gig it is – at some, you know the audience will be nice and there are friendly faces in the green room, but with others, it can be very different and Rachel will find she needs her space to think through her set. But as she mentioned earlier, once on stage, that anxiety disappears.

She went on to say that there is an assumption that all comedians are the life and soul of the party, but in reality that's not the case. There can be a clash of perceived status in green rooms sometimes, she said, and if you are considered the most successful, there is an assumption you won't get anxious and you almost have to act like the host – but in reality, if you're someone that gets nervous, that never really goes away. Rachel told us she looks back now to when she was starting out, and remembers wondering why the headliner seemed nervous – but she gets it now.

This was actually really reassuring to hear, and it certainly spoke to a lot of my own anxieties about social events and comedy. I did a gig recently in Bournemouth with two very experienced – but not necessarily famous – circuit comedians, and before the start of the show (which was a hard one, with a tough audience) both of them admitted they were nervous, and that the nerves never go away. It was a comfort that night (although it didn't save me from a difficult gig).

Rachel went on to offer us clear examples of how she uses what she knows about her anxieties to help her. She said that, for years, she wanted to think of herself as a free spirit, but as she got older, she realised that she actually craves structure. She finds it hard to write off the cuff; she needs to commit a day to writing. It's the same with gigs – some comedians she knows will happily accept last-minute bookings, but Rachel needs to have her schedule sorted weeks in advance so she can get her head around it. She never does last-minute shows, and if some details of a gig change on the night, like the promoter asks her to change the length of her set, or if the audience's chairs in the performance space have been set up in a way that isn't conducive to comedy (like not facing the stage, which can happen quite a lot) it can be challenging for her.

I decided to be a little bit more like both that TV presenter and Rachel after the episodes we recorded with them. I am trying to give less of a fuck about what other people think about me – both in terms of my work and also me in general. I am trying to just be myself, and whether people like me or not is for them to decide. I can only do me. I am also reading fewer comments online and choosing to concentrate on the good ones, giving my time and energy to them. And in social settings, I am trying to just relax and be a bit more myself. She arrived at our podcast unapologetically herself, and I want to do the same.

I am also trying not to say yes to every gig (although when you aren't offered that many, that can be hard). When Rachel said she only takes gigs she can properly prepare for, that really spoke to me. I also get nervous about last-minute things – not just gigs, but everything in life, really – and I need time to prepare and focus on what I'm going to do. If that is a way of approaching things that works for a successful comedian like Rachel, then that is something I can do, too. It's also a way of respecting yourself and your process – I don't need to say yes to things that knock me out of kilter; I can work in my own time and get the best out of myself as a result. Of course, this approach won't work for everyone reading this book, and if you are the sort of person who can say yes to things at the last minute, then go for it and fill your boots!

At the end of the day, knowing how to deal with things in a way that works around your own social anxieties will only help you to become happier and function better.

THE NUDGE UNIT

What it all comes down to, as everything does, is communication. Better communication can help reduce our anxiety. Fiona Murden explained to us why communication is absolutely key by referencing something called the 'Nudge Unit', which sounds like something out of an H. G. Wells novel, but is actually a real group that helps the UK government apply behavioural science to public policy. More formally known as the Behavioural Insights Team, it was formed by the coalition government in 2010 to specialise in nudge theory.

Popularised by economist Richard Thaler and Harvard professor Cass Sunstein in their 2008 book *Nudge: Improving Decisions about Health, Wealth, and Happiness*, this is the concept that the public can be 'nudged' into making the right economic and sociological decisions for themselves (and, essentially, cannot be trusted to make the right decisions on their own).

The Nudge Unit's biggest challenge since being formed was undoubtedly the COVID-19 pandemic of 2020, and their task was to help the government form messages to the public on how to stay safe. They didn't always get it right, however, and there was plenty of criticism for the mixed messaging Boris Johnson and his cabinet put out during the crisis. One of the things the Nudge Unit worked on was the messaging around washing your hands, and the singing of 'Happy Birthday' to make sure you did so for the recommended 20 seconds.*

I have my own thoughts on how the Nudge Unit did during the pandemic, but the very fact they exist proves how important communication is. If we tell people how we are feeling, what we want and what makes us uncomfortable, then surely we will have better experiences. Even the simple act of vocalising it will help. For example, we talked about feeling anxious before a performance. Communicating that anxiety to the people we work with might mean they make the environment more comfortable for us. Instead of having blank moments on our own, if we share them, we can turn them into great moments.

---

* https://www.instituteforgovernment.org.uk/explainers/nudge-unit.

Chapter 7:
Creativity

I have days where I don't give [creativity] a thought at all, but they're very few. I'm often thinking I could do with having a meeting, and obviously there will be patches in life when there is a financial necessity, though it's very rarely driven by that – it's just about being active and about, I suppose. It's about being wanted, an actor friend of mine said to me a year or so ago, when we talked about this kind of thing, and he was saying that people always talk about how hard it is being an actor because of the constant rejection. And he told me he didn't think that was the hard part, that it's not about the rejection, it's about being ignored – and actually 80–85 per cent of the time, you are just ignored.

Daniel Tuite

I knew from an early age that academia was not my bag and school was hard. Nothing seemed to be my thing – I was terrible at science, history, English and especially maths (I failed my GCSE twice!). And sport, which I loved, I was only ever average at.

This isn't me being down on myself; it was just a reality I kind of accepted early on: that I was wired differently. My neural pathways were clearly not connected up to whatever it is that helps you process algebra, understand the inner conflicts in Shakespeare's *Macbeth*, or kick a ball around.

So, when I left secondary school, I had one GCSE to my name, in English literature, and an overriding feeling of failure and worthlessness. I thought to myself, what does someone like me do now?

Although I was self-aware enough to know I was made differently, I still didn't know who I was, what my purpose was or where I was headed – other than backwards, to retake my exams.

But in much the way I'd approached school, I failed to take it all particularly seriously – and, inevitably, my lacklustre crusade to conform to what was expected of me ended in failure. I failed my retakes spectacularly and stopped turning up to lessons, finding the local pub a much better sanctuary during what was a rather rapid descent into chaos and self-loathing.

Then I was asked to leave college, because my attendance was such that there was no question of my carrying on. I never told anyone at home – my dad was never a sympathetic or encouraging kind of chap (see Chapter 8: Parenting) and he wouldn't have understood my plight. So I continued to get the train to college every weekday and I just hung out there, attempting to seem like I was still a student, with the full indignity of my situation masked by this pretence. I even got a job as an early-morning cleaner at the college so I could buy myself a little time to figure out what to do next. I was well and truly lost, a rudderless ship floating slowly away on an ocean of despair.

I felt worthless, like life had kicked me very hard, and while I was down on the floor, winded and writhing, it was kicking me again and again. Eventually, my dad found out I'd had to leave college and was suitably disappointed, but my life has a funny way of serving up the odd curveball.

In the process of trying to find some meaning in my life, during those mundane mornings of vacuuming classroom carpets and buffing parquet flooring in the assembly hall, I started to listen to myself for the first time. For so many years, I had been listening to everybody else, going along with what was required of me – to study, learn, be tested and then go and find my way in the world – but that path clearly wasn't my path. I found conventional learning hard and exams even harder. I just wasn't wired that way!

As I started to consider my future more deeply during those isolated early mornings spent buffing, I realised that I wanted to make something – to create. I can't tell you if it was one particular thing that sparked this eureka moment, but I can tell you that a growing desire to consume music, film, art and books had taken hold of me – especially music. I was ravenous for it! Those mornings spent cleaning allowed my mind to be fully quiet, the mundanity of the work gave my brain a chance to breathe, and with each breath came an intensity of belief that I did have a purpose, that I would do something meaningful, that I could progress in life without exams and qualifications – that there was another way.

I can say, hand on heart, that discovering my creativity truly saved my life.

———

Some months before this revelation, I found myself on the top of Seaford Head. I'd been through a period of heavy binge drinking, which led me to a very dark place – and that day, the drinking and my lack of purpose drove me to question my own existence. Sitting up there, having had half a bottle of Jack Daniel's some hours before, I genuinely considered ending it all.

I'm still not sure what stopped me from going through with it – fear mostly, I guess, and sobriety kicking back in, too. There was also a niggling sense of what I might be missing out on if I weren't here, and a feeling of there being something more to life. This something more is what continues to drive me forward today.

It's a time I think of a lot, with some gratitude that I made the decision I did, and that the glimmer of something more held me back. From that day on, one thought persisted: that I had to do something – something of significance, something to be proud of – that would outlive me.

This was my Peter-Parker-being-bitten-by-a-radioactive-spider moment, my Bruce-Banner-being-zapped-with-gamma-radiation incident, my own creative origin story.

I don't want it to seem like I'm trivialising this very dark episode in any way – it was probably the most challenging time I've ever experienced – but it is when we are at our most vulnerable that we start to truly feel a sense of what we can accomplish. It can emerge like a superpower, and a single moment of clarity can catapult you and give your life meaning again.

———

I took a lot away from our conversation with Sanjeev Bhaskar on the *Blank Podcast,* in particular when we discussed making decisions in difficult times. For him, we are defined by the future decisions we make rather than what's happened to us in the past. What you do next to overcome an obstacle – that's within your power, and that's on you. The question is, when you're making that decision, do you follow your instincts or your fear?

Instinct and fear serve as our guides in many different situations in life, and it can be hard to distinguish between them because they both speak with the same vocabulary, in the same accent, with the same cadence. But if you can listen to the one that comes from love, that's instinct, and that is the highest you.

This idea of being at a crossroads in our creative lives was something that came up when we spoke to Louis Theroux, who admitted, having recently done quite a few projects in a short period of time, that maybe he needed to take stock of things, as he was at a junction in his career. He said that trying new things had helped – for example, writing a book – but essentially, for him, going blank is an ever-present threat, something he sees as an adversary which keeps him on his toes.

Trying out lots of different things and taking stock of our lives, particularly our creative lives, is a chance to develop as individuals. This is something we should all be trying to do on a regular basis, by looking back on the path we have trodden and looking forward to what possibly lies ahead.

With this in mind, I considered what approaches might benefit my own life and work, and came up with a few jumping-off points that might be beneficial to others:

–   **Reflect** on the things you've done that have been successful or felt like an achievement, and see if there are elements you can replicate in other situations moving forward.

- **Assess** the various experiences and skills you have picked up along the way, and consider how these can be utilised in future projects.

- **Ask yourself** what you want to achieve and where you want to be in the future – find a focus, a goal. It can be large or small, but figuring out what it is will give your journey a purpose.

Another idea I liked was when Isy Suttie talked about doing more than one thing when trying to be creative. She mentioned that, when she's driving, she is, in a sense, being creative – and when you are having to make decisions all the time, like putting together a route or trying to park, you sometimes need to be extremely creative!

For Isy, another pastime is knitting, and she has come up with a process where she'll write for 45 minutes and then knit for quarter of an hour – and as she's knitting, her brain is subconsciously thinking over everything, so that when she goes back to write, she's often taken a mental leap that she wasn't even aware of. She also does this by playing Pac-Man. Taking a break to carry out a mundane, repetitive exercise can be far more beneficial than sitting in front of a blank screen or piece of paper.

This ties in to something I've begun to experiment with in my own creative life. In fact, when I was writing this book, I took regular short breaks to run around the garden, or make a cup of coffee, or play a game on my phone for ten minutes, and it's startling how much your mind starts to buzz with ideas in those moments.

Going back to our very first podcast, with Jon Ronson, he mentioned that one way he foils blank moments is to work on more than one project at a time. This approach works really well for him, and he's found it actually makes his creative life easier and more fruitful. But having more than one creative pursuit on the go doesn't always have a positive impact. For some, it can work the opposite way entirely.

This was certainly true for composer Peter Warlock, whose life took a desperate turn when he decided to pursue other creative endeavours ...

THE MUSIC CRITIC WHO KILLED A COMPOSER

On 17 December 1930, Peter Warlock was found dead in his flat in Chelsea, after taking his own life by way of lethal gas poisoning. In the years leading up to his death, the composer had found himself in a downward spiral of depression, brought on by his inactivity in creating new works.

Born Peter Heseltine in 1894 to fairly wealthy and well-connected parents, Arnold and Bessie, Warlock's early years were spent in Chelsea, where he first started to learn the piano. Peter was a highly intelligent individual and it was thought that academia would be his future path, but during his time at Eton, under the shadow of bullying, he discovered a love of music and it became a great solace to him, even an obsession. In particular, he studied the works of composer Frederick Delius.

Fed up with his life at Eton, Warlock decided to leave education for a year and travelled to Cologne in Germany to study piano at the Conservatory, and this is where he first began to write his own songs and dabble in journalism. A year later, he returned to London and, fuelled by passion and wanting to follow his heart, he decided to pursue a career in music. However, his mother had other ideas, and in the end Warlock went on to study classics at the University of Oxford.

This retreat back into academia was short-lived, and in 1915, with the help of a wealthy benefactor called Lady Emerald Cunard, Warlock landed a job at the *Daily Mail* as a music critic.

This new career allowed Warlock to pursue his obsession and be paid for it, and during his short time at the paper he wrote some thirty articles, but he started to see his pieces get cut and, in his frustration, he resigned.

During the following years, Peter Warlock spent time in Ireland and then Wales. His lack of income made life challenging, but during his time in Wales, he had an incredibly productive period of composing and writing, during which he produced some of his most famous pieces of music – as well as a biography of his hero, Delius.

Always a troubled individual, Warlock descended into severe depression in the years following his time in Wales. By the late 1920s, he was working as an editor and his creativity had all but dried up, though a minor revival occurred in 1930 when he wrote the piece 'The Fox'.

Back in London and living in a basement flat, Warlock hit rock bottom, and on the night of 16 December 1930, he placed his cat outside his room before turning on the gas that would take his life.

A creative mind bereft of creativity is a dark place, and for Peter Warlock it was something he could not continue to cope with. It seems he was never quite able to navigate the creative paths he trod. His critical work was his backup plan, his safety net when the creative work dried up, but it could be argued that immersing himself in writing about others led to the stifling of his own creativity – and it could also have been a constant reminder that this area of his life was in free fall. For many, a blank canvas is an opportunity to make something new; for others, it can be disheartening and at times even destructive.

BLANK

Nevertheless, Warlock's legacy lives on, and his work has become a huge influence on many contemporary composers. The Scottish author and composer Cecil Gray said of Warlock, 'In the memory of his friends, he is as alive now as he ever was when he trod the earth, and so he will continue to be until the last of us are dead.'

———

At times, the self-criticism and the pressure we put on ourselves to be creative can be hard to bear. Composer and producer Paul Pilot summed up his own attitudes towards creativity when we spoke about the way we sometimes focus too much on making our creative projects perfect, when actually a more holistic approach might yield better results.

Paul described it beautifully when he said that creativity is a bit like sport, but while in sport it's all about getting the ball in the back of a fixed net, with art you can move the net around to get the ball to go in. Some people still try to approach it with a sports mentality, but Paul believes in moving the net around – and afterwards, it's still perceived as the 'ball' landing beautifully. It's just a smarter way to do it.

I love this idea that we are more in control of what we are trying to achieve than we often give ourselves credit for. It's been a real eye-opener to hear that so many of our guests take a similar approach to Paul in their own work. It's an approach we can all take on board, whatever we do in life. I know I will.

JIM

I've always been a creative person, as far back as I can remember. I won a poetry competition in primary school for a poem about my hamster Hammy (the poem was more creative than the hamster's name). I wish I could remember it. I also used to make models out of Fimo (a child-friendly clay that was all the rage in the 1990s) – just silly little things like animals, dinosaurs, plates of food for some reason, and a hand doing a peace sign that my teacher bought from me for a pound (officially the first piece of art I ever sold).

My brother and I used to borrow our parents' camcorder to record our own football magazine show, splicing highlights from Channel 4's Italian football coverage – which we literally recorded by pointing the camcorder at the TV – and us presenting links in between goals. I seem to remember that I wrote the scripts and produced, and my brother Sebastian was just the talent – and a fairly diva-ish one, at that, if I'm being totally honest.

Then, in secondary school, I formed a three-person comedy troupe with my mates Robin and Sam, and wrote parodies of 'Wonderwall' and 'Three Lions'. We cut a three-track EP on cassette that Robin's mum helped us record, and I think she also designed the cover art. The 'Wonderwall' track was a piss-take of Millwall FC – hardly surprising as I supported (and still do!) their bitter rivals Crystal Palace – and the 'Three Lions' one was just a list of terrible footballers and why they were so terrible. I remember playing it to my best friend Callum at school, and forgetting he was a proud Scot until the song reached the line hammering Ally McCoist. I wasn't allowed to sit next to him on the bus home that day.

I also wrote my own football magazine during school, because I was bored and loved football and writing. When I got to A-Level Media Studies and the other students in my class were making leaflets for our coursework, I decided to produce a full-size, 30-page Crystal Palace fanzine. It was focused on the club's promotion-winning team of 1969, and my plan was to print 100 copies and actually sell them at a Palace match like a real fanzine. My teacher, Mrs Ruffle, was incredibly supportive, even though I suspect she thought I was hugely overambitious. But I somehow did it, complete with interviews with players from the team. I sold them at a game with my dad helping me out, and felt a huge sense of pride and accomplishment afterwards.

That feeling has followed me into my professional working life, and it dictates everything I do today, 19 years later. Making things has always given me this sensation. I can't quite describe it, but I guess I could say that it makes me feel whole. It makes me feel worthy and alive. If I'm having a bad day where I feel like the world is on my shoulders, and I'm so overwhelmed I can't see the wood for the trees, it's making something that makes me feel peaceful again. Some therapists and counsellors encourage clients to focus on one thing a day to help battle depression and anxiety, or other things that can stop you in your tracks. Self-care is massively important, and whether it's having a shower or journaling, focusing on yourself can get you on the right path. For me, what helps is making something. A problem I often run into is that everything I take on is huge.

But it doesn't have to be. I think we're actually not honest with ourselves a lot of the time about what we want to do and what we need to do. According to psychologist Fiona Murden, that lack of honesty with ourselves is something that everyone struggles with – even psychologists.

She explains that it is much easier to advise than it is to listen, and this is also true for someone like her, who is trained in listening and giving the right advice. She needs to feel busy and productive, even when her work or home life has calmed down a bit, which is why she is always giving herself projects to do. She says she used to feel guilty because she was trained in how to advise people, but would look at herself and see someone who was struggling.

CREATIVITY

It's all down to perspective, she adds, and filters. When you are focused on someone else's problems, your mind doesn't get clouded with negative thoughts of the self. It has clarity, and it filters out any negativity to focus on helping the other person. But when you are focused on yourself, those niggling thoughts come back and muddy the waters. It's the same with vocalising your problems and saying them out loud. That's why vocalising your problems can help, Fiona adds, because firstly, you are focusing on the things you are saying and secondly, if you say them to someone else, they can come at them with a fresh, focused, uncluttered approach.

Saying things out loud to make them seem more real is something my wife and I try to do at the start of every year, when we tell each other the things we want to achieve in the next 12 months. There is something about saying these things out loud to another person that somehow makes them more real, and makes you hold yourself accountable so you are more likely to meet them. Ours have included career milestones we've wanted to hit, family plans we've wanted to achieve, and life plans we've targeted – and so far, there isn't a single thing on our lists we haven't achieved after vocalising them to each other.

BLANK

MAN'S SEARCH FOR MEANING

When I was in my early twenties, I was enthusiastic but also quite pretentious. I would only be into bands no one else had heard of, and then, if they got big, I would never listen to them again. And I only really read books to look intelligent. I forced myself to get through *The Mayor of Casterbridge* by Thomas Hardy at one point. It took me eight months.

Anyway, one of the books I read to try to look important actually had a profound effect on me, and that was *Man's Search for Meaning* by Viktor Frankl.

The book is in two parts. The first is a diary-like retelling of
Frankl's time in four Nazi concentration camps during the
Second World War: Theresienstadt, Auschwitz, Kaufering and
Türkheim. It includes graphic depictions of prisoners fighting
for scraps of food, and none of the horrors he witnessed and
experienced are glossed over. Frankl is as honest as he can be
as he paints a picture of what life was like for the millions of
Jewish people who were taken prisoner. It is a powerful and
harrowing read.

The second half of the book takes what he has described in the
first half and begins to unpick it all using the psychotherapeutic
method he created. That method sees people find a purpose
in their life – their figurative and literal 'search for meaning' –
and then visualise the outcome of that purpose with as much
imagination as possible.

The book sets out to answer the question: 'How was everyday
life in a concentration camp reflected in the mind of the average
prisoner?' According to Frankl, the way a prisoner imagines the
future affects their longevity, and he has facts and figures to
back that up.

My unlearned brain translates Frankl's method as a form of
visualisation, and that is something that a lot of people use
today – particularly sports people – to help them bring their
goals and targets to life as a way of achieving them. Of course,
trophies and championships pale into insignificance next to
surviving concentration camps.

Frankl took a methodical and scientific approach to the horrors
he saw, and his theory of logotherapy is regularly put up against
Nietzschean doctrine and Freudian principles. As soon as I read
that, I knew I was Team Frankl all day long. Freud and Nietzsche
can do one.

Logotherapy is founded upon the belief that striving to find meaning in life is the most important motivating force for humans. That is a powerful conclusion, and yet it makes complete and utter sense to me. More so than anything else I've ever read in my life. And it doesn't just make sense to me on a superficial level, but in a deep, inward way that I can actually feel. When I have a purpose, I *feel* better. It's that sensation I mentioned earlier that I can't quite explain – I just know I am happier, more peaceful and like a complete human when it happens.

That Frankl detailed exactly how his theories helped him survive surely the worst atrocity human beings have forced on each other only makes his theory more profound and meaningful to me. Obviously, it makes my visualisations of 30-page fanzines with 50-year-old footballers talking about kicking a ball around a pitch seem meaningless in comparison, but it's important to realise that purpose is relative. One man's purpose might seem silly to another, but it is his and his alone – and how much it matters to him is what's important.

BLANK

———

We talk about things that drive us on the podcast quite a bit, and the idea of using purpose to drive creativity came up when we spoke to David Baddiel. A big Chelsea fan, he referenced a former Gunners player called Gus Caesar, who is mentioned in Nick Hornby's *Fever Pitch.*

In the book, Hornby talks about Caesar's career. He was a defender who rose through Arsenal's youth ranks in the early 1980s, and by the middle of the decade, he had worked his way into the first team, turning pro in 1984. No mean feat, considering Arsenal were one of England's most famous and biggest clubs. But the problem for Caesar was that he was, to put it bluntly, just never quite good enough for Arsenal.

He struggled to find form, the fans started getting on his back, and even opposition players were taking the mickey out of him during games. Caesar left Arsenal in 1991 and disappeared from top-tier football. What Hornby brilliantly explains is that Caesar must have been absolutely brilliant at football as a kid, the best player at his school and on his youth team, and he no doubt felt like he was absolutely destined to be a footballer. 'You trust that feeling with your life, you feel the strength and determination it gives you coursing through your veins like heroin ... and it doesn't mean anything at all,' Hornby writes, devastatingly.

Baddiel added that Giles and I might have assumed that it was his destiny to be a comedian, but he believed it was more a matter of luck and uncertainty – and to some extent, fate and timing.

It did make me worry if I was maybe comedy's Gus Caesar: great at open-mic level, but destined never to be good enough for the very top. Even so, I'd probably take Caesar's career – he played professional football for another 14 years after leaving Arsenal. But David is sort of right, Caesar's destiny was never to be a footballer – and he knew it. He has since been quoted* as saying he never really wanted to be a footballer, and actually wanted to go into business – and that is what he does today. His house was never filled with football memorabilia, it was just something he was good at. Well, okay at. Like me and journalism.

So, to me, this story still has a happy ending. Just because Gus Caesar didn't have the career in football that many people wanted him to (or wanted for themselves), he has achieved his goal, his purpose, his meaning. It was his script, not anyone else's. And he still knew what he wanted, even when lots of other people had mapped his life out as going somewhere different.

---

* https://www.hamhigh.co.uk/sport/football/arsenal/gus-caesar-i-still-have-nightmares-about-wembley-final-disaster-1-627788.

Is it the same for me? Well, I've never made a career-defining mistake in whatever comedy's equivalent of Wembley is (the Comedy Store?) or journalism's equivalent of Wembley (the *Financial Times*?), but I know what I want to do – and no one else's definition of my career is going to stop me. I will actually use Gus Caesar as an inspiration from now on, because I think his career is actually a success story and not the tragedy everyone thinks it is.

————

This idea of knowing your future, seeing it and making it happen is visualisation. This is a tool that a lot of sports people use to try to deflect pressure before a big game so they can concentrate on the moment at hand. But when Nick Faldo, arguably England's best-ever golfer, joined us on the podcast, he revealed he went even further than just visualising his game.

Faldo, who won six major golf tournaments between 1987 and 1996, said he had the ability to turn everything off when the pressure was getting too much. He talked about his infamous win at the Open Championship in 1992, when, leading on the final day, it all started falling apart. He told himself to just forget everything that had happened so far – the four days of rounds leading up to the final day, all the practice sessions, all the years of golf before this moment. None of it mattered. He started all over again, near the end of his final round, with just four holes to go. All his focus was on those four holes.

He said that was a tactic he often used. When he had a bad hole during a tournament, he used to pretend that on the five-minute walk to the next hole, an entire fortnight had passed. The odds of you still being annoyed at something silly you did two weeks ago are usually miniscule, so pretending all that time had passed helped him to forget about it and concentrate on what was next.

This is such a fascinating yet simple technique that I think a lot of people, in any walk of life, can relate to and use.

Faldo also used to take himself out of big tournaments mentally and picture himself back on the driving range or putting green, imagining himself just practising with no pressure. He would try to replicate the feeling he had when he was just hitting balls for fun rather than competing in a major tournament. He would simplify the language between himself and his pioneering caddy, Fanny Sunesson, who was the first female caddie in world professional golf. It was very direct information:
'What do I want?'
'To hit the ball 150 yards.'
'Okay.'

He used to give himself clear instructions going into each day of a tournament. If he needed to claw back four shots, he would tell himself, 'I am going to win by four shots today.' Saying it out loud, like Fiona told us earlier, and visualising himself doing it helped him make it a reality.

At the Masters in 1996, his last major win, he was facing off against his best friend, Greg Norman. He imagined himself turning to face the course, not looking at anyone – least of all Greg – and hitting what he needed to win. Faldo shot a 67, the best score of the day, to overturn a six-stroke deficit, tying the biggest lead ever blown in a PGA Tour tournament.

I have to admit I think I do a form of visualisation without even realising. When I am playing football, I sometimes find myself, during a game, imagining scoring a winning goal. (Obviously it becomes harder to manifest that visualisation when I spend most of the time on the bench.) When I do eventually get playing time, and even get into a position to score, I'm never thinking about what's happening. I'm just doing. And maybe that's something that I can take into my professional working life.

I really like the idea of resetting like Nick Faldo used to do during a game of golf when he tuned out the previous days of play. Thinking about past wins and defeats at work – things we have done well, things we have done badly – can take up valuable creative time, and I am definitely guilty of doing it a lot.

———

What I have to remind myself to do is to keep making things, as that's my fuel. It's what keeps me going. But maybe if I made some small things from time to time, I might be able to supercharge that fuel, that purpose, more easily – rather than getting myself bogged down with big projects and perfection. Art doesn't have to be perfect or big, it just needs to be enough to keep you going.

It's so easy to be hard on yourself when you sit down to write and that big blank page stares back at you on your laptop. Especially if you lead a busy life, you have kids, or you are being creative in your spare time, outside of your normal job. That time to be creative can seem like sand slipping through your fingertips, and unless you're bashing out the next Pulitzer Prize–winning novel, it's easy to beat yourself up. I certainly do that, and that's why making this podcast has been a real help. Hearing that some of the most successfully creative people out there struggle too has been a huge relief. It isn't just me!

But how do we switch on creativity? Well, the answer is we never really switch it off. As Isy Suttie told us earlier in this chapter, you are actually always being creative, even when you don't realise it. Every decision you make is a form of creativity, and there is actual science to back that up.

When psychologist Fiona Murden chatted to us about the science behind blank moments, she revealed some really interesting stuff about switching on creativity. She said that,

even for the most prolific creative people, who from the outside
seem to be able to turn creativity on and off at will, it actually
takes them hours and hours to come up with a single line.
People only ever see the end result, but the reality is not like
that at all.

She referenced some creatives in the fashion industry she
had worked with who seem to be able to just switch on their
creativity, but what is actually happening is that their brains
have been trained to work on designs and ideas constantly, even
when they don't put pen to paper – so when they eventually do
sit down to work, it all comes tumbling out. They are constantly
thinking about being creative – almost daydreaming about it.
She added that there was a piece of research carried out in
Chile on schoolchildren, and it showed that the children that
were able to consciously switch in and out of daydreaming
were also able to be more creative.

As someone who probably daydreams about 90 per cent of
the time, this was such a relief. To know that, actually, during
those times when I thought I was wasting my day, I am actually
still being creative – and that, just because I am not sitting
down at my laptop banging out word after word after word,
it doesn't mean that I'm not working on something. The more
I thought about this after our episode with Fiona, the more I
realised that I am *always* thinking of ideas. In fact, I find it hard
to turn them off. It actually annoys me at times that I can't
stop thinking about certain sketch or stand-up ideas, or the
clothes I want to buy and match with other clothes, or the
colour I want to paint the walls in our spare room … but I
shouldn't chastise myself. This is creativity, and it actually
comes from a place of curiosity.

They say curiosity killed the cat, and I hate that phrase.
Is it supposed to put us off being curious? To curtail our
adventurous side? Because that is the side that we need to

look after. Being curious is amazing. And, again, there is science to back that up, as Fiona Murden explained.

Curiosity, she told us, has driven us as a species to evolve as much as we have. It has become part of who we are, and there is a huge amount of research showing how it can actually prolong life. There was one study, Fiona said, that was carried out over several years, and it showed that people who are more curious live longer. She added that curiosity is also incredibly good for our mental well-being, and has been shown to be good for physical health as well, because it is such an innate part of who we are.

That makes total sense, but it does seem a bit overwhelming, so it was a relief when Fiona said that it doesn't have to be a big thing – it can be curiosity about why your baby isn't going to sleep and what their body is doing; it can be noticing something in the corner of a window you haven't noticed before. It's basically about being observant of what's going on, and in a way, it is a bit like being a detective.

Fiona referenced the example of Nelson Mandela, who was imprisoned for 27 years. When he was locked up, he was incredibly curious about loads of different things. He did a law degree, he wrote to many different world leaders, and he read a huge amount about people who were vital to different events in history. If you look at anyone who is prominent or respected, you'll see someone who is curious, Fiona added.

This can help with trying to understand other people, especially those who think differently to us or hold opposing views. Being curious about what they say and why they say it is an opportunity to find out why they reacted like that. Fiona also thinks we can all afford to be more curious about ourselves. Not necessarily through introspection or self-analysis; they can be unhelpful because we end up overanalysing. But being curious and stepping back and wondering why you reacted to something in a certain way can be massively beneficial, she adds.

Okay, I'm not quite Nelson Mandela, but then did Nelson Mandela ever write a rap about being vegetarian? Probably not. And I love the idea of using curiosity to improve ourselves, asking questions about why we do certain things and how we can do them differently. I think that if we lose our curiosity, we lose a massive part of ourselves that makes us special. I've tried to be even more curious since the episode with Fiona, and I've realised that I'm not even sure that's possible. Even when researching this chapter, I ended up down a Wikipedia wormhole that saw me spending a good hour or so reading about lime quarries (good luck working out how I got there), but I did learn a lot about limestone – and who knows when that information will come in handy?!

Chapter 8:
Parenting

If you wrap someone in cotton wool, yeah they don't get hurt – but they also don't know that they can get hurt and survive.

Angela Scanlon

A chapter on parenting is like all the other chapters in this book rolled into one. Imposter syndrome, public failure, a lack of sleep, social anxiety, and many, many blank moments are only some of the issues you face as a parent. The feelings that being a mum or a dad bring up include many of those we've discussed in the book so far, feelings which regularly come up on the podcast, only they are weirdly heightened by it not being about you but about this tiny human you have produced and introduced to the world.

And yet despite our kids making us feel more anxious than we ever thought possible, more embarrassed than anything we've done ourselves, more of a failure than ever before, and more of an imposter than any other previous life event, they also seem to manage to be the antidote to all those crushing feelings. One cuddle or smile from our little monsters at the end of a long day can make all those worries – which we not only have about ourselves, but about them, too – completely disappear. There aren't really any other things in life that can be the cause and cure of so many of life's most crippling emotions.

I come from an Irish Catholic family, so I have quite a few first cousins (20, to be exact) and even more second cousins (somewhere around 100, my dad isn't even sure). My dad is one of seven and has six sisters – three younger, three older. I have absolutely no idea how he survived, to be honest, but now, since having a child of my own, I've come to recognise the extent of what my Irish grandparents must have gone through in having their seven children. I could write a whole book about the emotions that my wife and I have experienced since our daughter was born 18 months ago. I can't imagine going through that SEVEN times!

Weirdly, when we had Stephen Mangan on the podcast, it became apparent that we had almost identical families.

BLANK

His parents had come over from Ireland just as my grandparents had; we both had tons of first cousins on account of big Catholic families (52 in his case); and while his dad's family had settled in London, his mum's family moved to Chichester, which is where my parents moved to a few years ago. Like Stephen, family was a big part of growing up for me. I was lucky that I had a supportive family who would always let me explore whatever stupid thing I was into at the time and never discouraged me. I didn't realise it then, but I was picking up clues as to how to be a good parent from my mum and dad. And now I'm a parent myself, I'm trying desperately to be an equally good example for my daughter.

Parenting has been something of a journey for me since we started the podcast. When we launched our first episode in September 2018, I was a married man with no children; and at the time of writing this book, I am still a married man (thankfully!), with an 18-month-old daughter. For my wife Miranda and me, our entire journey of getting pregnant and having the baby happened alongside my journey on the podcast, and so I am always keen to hear what sort of role our guests' parents had played in their lives.

Some people are heavily influenced by their parents, like poet Michael Rosen, who lit up when we asked about his childhood. He referenced his book *So They Call You Pisher!* when he talked about his parents, Connie and Harold, who were clearly big characters, not just in the Rosen household, but in their local community of Pinner in north-west London. They would organise Communist Party branch meetings in the house, and members would come round while little Michael hid on the stairs watching it all unfold (having pretended to go to bed). There was lederhosen-wearing Max, and tall Len who worked on the Comet jet airliners for BOAC. It's no wonder Michael grew up with hundreds of characters in his head for his stories and poetry.

Another guest whose parents have had a huge influence on them is the multi-talented Ben Bailey Smith, aka Doc Brown. He is an actor, comedian, writer and musician who comes from a family where all the children ended up working in the creative industries – but that didn't come from his parents. He told us that, despite having a sister who is an acclaimed author, a younger brother who is a musician and writer, a half-brother who is a musician and a half-sister who is a painter, his parents were not particularly creative. This abundance of creativity was just something that was in the kids for some reason, and was clearly going to come out in one form or another. However, things might have gone differently for Ben – his dream when he was younger was to become either an actor or a milkman. He liked the idea of being his own boss and having a sense of duty to the people he would deliver milk to, and he wanted to cruise around town in his milk float.

The episodes with Michael and Ben – and many other episodes too – got me thinking about what sort of dad I would be, and the kind of influence parents have on their kids, and how parenting can be one big blank moment. At the time of recording those episodes, my wife was pregnant with our daughter. No one really knows what they are doing, and the whole parenting experience, for me, has felt like constantly being on work experience with a tiny, demanding boss who throws you into new situations every day to see if you sink or swim – never praising you, often chastising you, and changing their mind as to what they want on an hourly basis. If this was an internship, I'd have quit ages ago.

But there are rewards – not just in the smiles and hugs that get increasingly common the further into the work experience you get (inappropriate from a boss really, but never mind), but also the fact that you are helping shape a person's whole outlook on life. Clearly, Michael Rosen's parents helped him to be inquisitive and question things, to go against the flow and to back himself and, most importantly, to be creative.

I realise now I am a dad that I learned my whole outlook on life from my parents – through the things they did and said. I learned the importance of support from my dad, who has always been there for me, no matter what new career I've chosen every two years or so. I also learned how to be logical in the face of crisis or blankness from him, and the importance of preparation. And from my mum, I learned unwavering compassion. I could write a whole book full of examples of her compassion and how she helps others, and as a mum she was no different. I've tried to be the same as a parent since our daughter was born.

They taught me these things in the good times and the bad, and I certainly brought my parents many, many instances of the latter – from falling down marble staircases as a child when we lived in Spain and cracking my head open (twice), to cracking it open again by falling through a French window as a 20-year-old after having one too many sangrias. I often didn't know what I was doing as a young adult; I was confused and angry and sad, and probably very hard to live with. But they coached me through a lifetime of mistakes and blank moments, and helped mould me into a somewhat-functioning member of society, who still cries and falls over from time to time. Now that the responsibility of parenting has been passed on to me, I'm hoping that I can coax my daughter through the next 20 years' worth of blank moments in her life.

But it isn't just my mum and dad who have influenced me as a parent. I'm lucky enough to have the kindest person I've ever met as my wife and team-mate in this parenting game. She may not realise it, but Miranda has a huge influence on me every day – with pretty much everything. Whether it's constantly playing Jamie Cullum on Google Home, which I moan about (while I have secretly added lots of his songs to my Spotify playlists and listen to them on my own); or the way she treats other people with compassion, often putting others' needs ahead of her own.

As a mum, she is so brilliant and it makes me want to be a good dad, too. I think it's important to recognise those influences in life that aren't just the obvious ones.

With parenting, it could be your partner, or your friends, or the guy from the corner shop and the way he talks about his kids. We are all out here giving each other bits of advice whether we mean to or not and it's vital to be open to them.

I have been always terrified about the responsibility of being a dad, from the moment Miranda fell pregnant, but when we met Ellie Gibson from the brilliant and hilarious Scummy Mummies, I realised I was on the right path. She told us that terrified is the best way to be, and that the people she's seen come a cropper are the ones who think they know exactly what being a parent is going to be like. Especially when they think it's going to be all lollipops and rainbows, because it really isn't most of the time. I think that applies to all of life, to be honest.

BLANK

GILES

On 6 July 1943, during the allied invasion of Sicily, my grandfather Charles Phillips's plane was shot down. My father would have been just two years old at the time. It's a tragic moment in my father's life that I have only just recently started to appreciate the full extent of – but back to that later.

Parenting? Where do I start? It's a true behemoth of a subject, entwined with so many aspects of our lives. It's a conversation starter, a source of empathy, and an all-singing, all-dancing cause of so many wonderful emotions – of pure joy and unadulterated happiness and pride – as well as those dreaded feelings of guilt and terror, anger and frustration. It's the most beautiful thing, and also the most challenging.

The moment my wife and I decided to have a child was while we were sitting on the number 12 bus from Seaford to Eastbourne, discussing what the next few years of our lives might hold for us. Neither of us was following any sort of particular career trajectory at that point; I was managing a toy shop and Michelle was a teaching supervisor. We were pursuing creative ventures on the side – I was in a band and Michelle was a trained interior designer – but neither of us was progressing with our dreams, and it felt like the perfect time to try to live out another dream: to become parents.

There are thousands of books on parenting, and not a single one of them will truly prepare you or guide your own experience of becoming a parent. The range of emotions alone would need a multitude of editions, and of course there is no one book for your own child! And something they also don't often mention is the time it might take to fall pregnant.

My wife and I had conceived a dream, an ideal, a parenting utopia. We talked baby names, bedroom colours, pushchairs, eco-nappies, breastfeeding, Dr Spock ... but there was one fairly major stumbling block: we were finding it hard to actually conceive.

At first we thought it was timing, that maybe we weren't syncing up properly, so we doubled our efforts; and without wanting to be too graphic (this isn't that kind of book), what was incredibly fun and pleasurable became slightly robotic and clinical. We were trudging up to the peak of our conception Everest, and like most explorers who find themselves stuck, we had to figure out whether there might be another route to take.

So, we booked an appointment with our GP. We needed expert assistance; we were a year into this dream of ours, and it was slowly disappearing. We were asking ourselves big questions – what if I was firing blanks (always on brand), what if my wife's reproductive equipment was faulty, what if we couldn't ever have children?

It felt like a biological failure on both our parts, and all those feelings that come with any moment of failure were joined by the potential loss of our wished-for outcome. Our longing to become parents had grown more and more intense as the prospect seemed to slip further away.

But remember that failure often lies in the eye of the beholder. Failure isn't where the story ends; it's not the concluding chapter or the end credits. The moment failure appears on your horizon is the start of an opportunity to look for ways to succeed.

Of course, this is not an easy thing to do, and emotions do get the better of us. For my wife and me, it was an incredibly challenging time. Our GP tried to reassure us and give us the possible scientific reasons, but at this stage it was a case of hold tight and keep trying.

This was to be the first of many parenting blank moments.

Anguish turned to sadness and an acknowledgement that maybe it wasn't meant to be for us, and we started to consider alternative avenues through which we could become parents should our fears turn out to be true. But so often in life, amazing things happen when you least expect them, and having booked further appointments with medical professionals to see what was going on, my wife then informed me her period was late.

All that uncertainty about whether we would be able to conceive made the moment when the two lines showed up on the pregnancy test all the more jubilant. We were so grateful that we were able to have children after all, and it's something I've never taken for granted, knowing many people, for whatever reason or circumstance, who haven't been able to. It must be unbelievably painful, and my thoughts are always with those people.

And so, for me, being a parent is a privilege and a gift, and even in its most challenging moments, it continues to amaze me, enthral me, and teach me to be the best person I can possibly be. And to be the parent I never had.

THE ABSENT PARENT

For many years, writers have used an absent parent to drive their protagonist's narrative – from Charles Dickens through to Roald Dahl and J. K. Rowling – and the same theme is seen in films like *Star Wars* and *E.T.* All across these well-known fictional worlds, we have seen our heroes dealing with a childhood bereft of one or both parents. Indeed, in children's literature in particular, there are a lot of deceased parents.

So why do creators of these stories use this device so often? Well, it often allows for several tropes to develop within a story – from boy wizards to timid workhouse orphans, the conceit of being parentless gives the creator the freedom and reason to put their character in all manner of situations. Without any parents getting in the way, their adventures are limitless. These characters have to learn and grow and develop as people on their own, using their own smarts, instincts and ingenuity. There is less hand-holding.

In books like *The Hunger Games*, the death of a parent forges certain aspects of a character's personality. After the loss of her father, the protagonist Katniss has to take on a parenting role, and this results in a protectiveness over her sister, which is what really drives the entire plot. And this theme appears in some of the most famous fairy tales too.

Think of Cinderella – her father's untimely death leads to a life of abuse at the hands of her stepmother and stepsisters, and in stories like this, the conceit gives the ultimate pay-off in the finale, when the baddies get their comeuppance and our unfortunate protagonist gets their version of a happy-ever-after.

All stories require conflict, and what bigger conflict than the loss of a loved one at a young age?

Sometimes the idea that the hero ever had parents in the f irst place can be sidelined or forgotten, but the best stories invoke the larger impact the loss of a parent has on its characters. Just think of Harry Potter, and how his parents become a significant part of the evolution of the series, allowing for a more intense emotional arc when the story enters its final stages.

Like most common story tropes, the idea of the absent parent is one that has stood the test of time in fiction, because even those readers who have not themselves experienced the loss of a parent can still empathise with the feelings that this scenario conjures up.

———

When we spoke to actor Rufus Sewell on the *Blank Podcast*, he talked at length about his early life and the impact it has had on him. His family were very poor. His mum and dad were separated, and his dad was financially worse than useless, so Rufus's mum had various jobs and she basically brought them up on her own – even more so after his dad died when Rufus was ten.

Rufus recalled that his mum had a vegetable round. She'd purloined this London black cab, which she drove without the taxi sign on, and she'd go and get cheap or free vegetables from Kew markets – she'd hoodwink the barrow boys – and then she'd sell whatever wasn't rotten to a little collection of friends and local housewives, and the family would keep what was left. So his mum, this shoeless six-foot woman with wild hair, would turn up in a black cab full of rotting pomegranates to pick him up from school …

Rufus admitted that he was a bit of a truant at school. He said that when people asked him if it might be a psychological reaction to his dad's death, he'd just say 'Fuck off!' – but on reflection, they were probably right.

What Rufus said on the podcast about the loss of a parent and its impact on childhood really connected with me. Loss and absenteeism were very much at the forefront of my own family background. But unlike some of the people we read about in fiction, in real life it takes a long time to truly come to terms with it and start to find your way.

My dad didn't know how to parent. In fact, he was shit at it. At the age of 41, he found himself a widower and father to two young boys, my mother having recently passed away after years living with terminal leukaemia. All the time she was around, my dad was able to amble along, often passing us off to grandparents when he needed to be with my mother, or at work, council meetings and (of course) the pub. Once my mum was no longer with us, my dad went into supersonic absentee-parent mode, the pub replacing practically everything else in his life.

Being so young, I often made excuses for my dad – in my own head and to everyone else. 'He's hurting,' I thought, 'he's not good at dealing with life.' And maybe those things are true, but having lost his own father at such a young age, maybe it's that he never had the requisite skills and emotional responsibility to raise children in the first place.

I won't lie, I pined for my dad – or should I say *a* dad – in the same way that perhaps he had pined for his own father (or *a* father). But booze became his family and his significant other, and it was a relationship that would eventually take his life.

I'm not going to make excuses for my dad any more – he totally dropped the ball. Being a parent myself now, I know that the levels of patience, dedication and empathy required just weren't in him, and he was too selfish a human to fully commit to being a parent. But as the years have gone on, I have grown to understand why that may have been the case for him – and I wasn't going to allow myself to follow suit. I'm a different person to my dad, I know that, but the idea of being everything to my own children that he wasn't to me has been an inspiration in a very strange, fucked-up, dysfunctional-family sort of way.

A beautiful quote that has stuck in mind ever since I first read it is one by Ida B. Wells: 'The way to right wrongs is to turn the light of truth upon them.' Being able to reflect on and admit to the mistakes of the past, and truly accept when those we love are at fault, means we can move forward. And that's the biggest lesson I've learned. Having a bad parent has helped me to become a better one.

Chapter 9:
Education, Mentors and Careers

In my school year, all the clever people were trouble makers and all the trouble makers were clever. I never knew when to stop, even if you know the teacher was getting angry I'd always be the one who carried on doing it. That was my thing. I knew that I could make people laugh, but mainly by doing something they wouldn't do.

Kevin Day

We have to look back some three thousand years to see the roots of mentoring: in Homer's *Odyssey*, the character of Mentor was entrusted with the care of Telemachus, Odysseus's son, while he headed off for some fisticuffs in Troy. Mentor wasn't specifically a sage or even particularly effective; he was basically just Odysseus's mate doing him a solid.

The use of the word 'mentor' to mean a person of guidance and influence in a younger person's life didn't really start to emerge until 1699, when the French writer Fénelon published a novel called *Les Aventures de Télémaque*. It features Mentor as teacher to Telemachus, not just as a glorified babysitter – and the eventual plot twist involves him dropping his disguise and revealing himself to be Minerva, the goddess of wisdom. (As plot twists go, this wasn't exactly up there with the likes of Keyser Söze or *The Sixth Sense*, but it is interesting nonetheless.) Fénelon's depiction of Mentor laid the path for the modern context of the word, used increasingly in the workplace from the 1970s, when business leaders adopted it as part of the process of inspiring and training junior members of staff.

Mentoring has evolved and now takes on different forms depending on the person or industry. A mentor can be any trusted advisor, teacher, boss, relative or friend whose wisdom and experience can help those willing to listen.

If I'd been asked before we started this podcast who my mentors were, I probably would have said I'd never had any. But over the course of the conversations we've had, we've spoken to many guests who have one or more people in their lives who have played a significant part in their journeys and what they have achieved. For some, like myself, it isn't always obvious who their mentor is, and they've had to reflect on specific instances when someone said or did some momentous thing that steered their lives in a particular direction.

The first time I really started to think about my own significant moments and influences was when we spoke to Amanda Abbington, who told us about one of her teachers at drama school. She said how she'd learned so much from this one man, John Gardiner, who would have great people coming in, giving talks and doing workshops.

It felt like we were discovering who Amanda's mentor was at the same time that she was, and actually this often happens on the pod. Certainly, listening back on all the episodes while writing this book has inspired me to reflect on those people who have come in and out of my own life and changed its course for the better: the teacher who gave me praise when no one else did; the college peers who encouraged me to start a band; my wife, who continues to mentor me daily; and also every single guest from the podcast, each of whom has given me something to take on board, and helped me to develop as a creative and a person.

Actor, writer and producer Jim Piddock alluded to his experiences of being mentored, and talked about how honesty and gratitude play such a vital part of the mentor/mentee relationship. Jim thinks it's really important to be honest – there were a couple of people who did it for him when he was younger, and it's something Jim has never forgotten. In particular, there was a writer on his first pilot who was very helpful to him. Jim had said he was interesting in writing, and this writer had invited him over to where he was working on set, and they'd chatted for over an hour about the craft. This writer told Jim all about the process and the business side, and he was just so encouraging.

Jim was very grateful, and a year after this conversation, he called the writer to let him know that what he had done had meant so much to him. That conversation had changed Jim's life, especially in terms of his career as a writer. Jim truly thinks that it is so important to give others your time; a few kind words of encouragement can go a long way to helping others, and it doesn't cost anything.

MR MIYAGI: THE ULTIMATE MENTOR

Cinema has a knack for coming up with the best and worst kinds of mentors. For every Mr Keating from *Dead Poets Society*, we get a Tyler Durden from *Fight Club*; for every Obi-Wan, there is an evil Emperor Palpatine. The mentor – very much like absent parents – is a trope that is seen again and again in the movies: the true coming-of-age story often cannot exist without one. I mean, what would have happened to Daniel LaRusso without Mr Miyagi? He'd just have been fairly shit at karate, one presumes.

So the role of the mentor is a vital one, but when we consider mentors, we must also consider the part played by the mentee – or 'protégé' is probably a better word. What would Mr Miyagi have been like without his Daniel-san? Well, he would have spent far more time pruning his bonsai trees and worrying about all the chores he needed to do around the house – things he was able to complete with Daniel's help. (For anyone who is reading this and hasn't seen *The Karate Kid*, I'm afraid spoilers are coming.)

You could be mistaken in thinking that Daniel's labour in exchange for a few karate tips is a plot device to show how resilience is king, but what it actually shows is Miyagi's methodical and introspective approach to mentoring. It's not all showy and shouty, he's not attempting to pump Daniel up; he's showing him the subtle ways in which we can graduate the school of hard knocks.

BLANK

The plot of the film is a familiar one: new kid from a broken family arrives in town, falls foul of the local bullies, who mentally and physically abuse him, and is constantly reminded of his not-so-great new life. Karate is the vehicle used to deliver a coming-of-age story and a tool to change the protagonist's life, but at its heart, the film is a story of the friendship and relationship between mentor and student.

Miyagi has his own demons – during the middle part of the film, he opens up about the loss of his wife and son in childbirth at an internment camp while he was serving in Europe during the Second World War. With Daniel being a child of divorce who lives apart from his father, a paternal bond is formed between the two. Daniel is just as important to Miyagi, and through Miyagi's teachings, they both come to realise the personal balance and equilibrium that karate brings. As viewers, we see that the very best mentors will have experienced hardships – indeed, this is often why they are able to pass on their knowledge from a place of authority. As Albert Einstein reportedly once said, 'The only source of knowledge is experience.'

There are many lessons to be taken from watching *The Karate Kid*: learn to take the knocks that life throws at you; cheaters never prosper; practice makes perfect; revenge is never a good idea – but the one that has stayed with me is to always listen to the humble mentor.

At the very end of the film, there is a big karate tournament, a chance for Daniel to shine and prove himself to his bullies, who all belong to the local military-style dojo run by one of cinema's biggest pricks, John Kreese. In the penultimate bout, Kreese tells one of his students to 'sweep the leg' – an illegal move that would ultimately render his opponent, in this case Daniel, unable to continue given the severity of the damage it would cause.

Well, suffice to say, this dastardly strategy doesn't pay off, and through his own mentor's worldly advice – and some implausible voodoo healing techniques – Daniel comes through it all to win, with a very proud Mr Miyagi beaming at his young apprentice from the sidelines just before the credits roll.

The ultimate mentors provide their students with the very best life lessons and shepherd them through their darkest (and blankest) moments, but they are also not afraid to show their own weaknesses. And in the case of Mr Miyagi, they are very good at manipulating their teachings in ways that mean their students end up doing all their domestic chores. Paint the fence, sand the floor, wax on, wax off – the man was a genius!

———

Ellen Elizabeth Carpenter – or Nanny Queenie, as I more fondly knew her – never realised she was a mentor, but she was, to all intents and purposes, my Mr Miyagi.

When my mum died, it was obviously felt by the entire family, but none more so than by my Nanny Queenie. Losing your only child must be unbearable, and being a parent, I can't even begin to fathom the feelings that must come with that kind of loss.

Queenie was every bit what we imagine a grandmother of a certain era to be – a roast-dinner-making, scone-baking, housecoat-wearing, all-singing, all-dancing family matriarch, topped off with a rinse and set and horn-rimmed glasses. But there was always something very different about Queenie, and she had a very quiet, reserved and sensitive demeanour. That's my memory of her at least; my brother, who is older than me and lived with her for many years, may have a different perception, but to me she was the very epitome of kindness.

After my grandfather passed away, I spent weekends at
Queenie's flat, and these one-to-one times with her are some
of my very favourite memories from childhood. She would
teach me things – always so attentive when showing me new
card games, always patient when allowing me to join in with
baking, never a cross word when I messed about or got on her
nerves. She was every inch the empathetic parent. It makes me
emotional just writing this, because she made me strive to be
the best person I can possibly be.

An instance that is still so clearly etched in my mind is a time
when a friend and I got caught pinching some Panini stickers
for our Transformers sticker album from the local newsagent's.
It was the first and last time I ever stole anything, and it's
something I still feel extremely guilty about.

My dad ranted and raved – his go-to was always rage and shame
– and he told me that I'd let the family down. A few days later,
I went to Queenie's house. I knew she would be disappointed
in me, but as always with her, she did something surprising.
She took me aside while she was peeling spuds, put her arm
around me, squeezed me tight, and said, 'It's okay, tell me
what happened.'

I proceeded to offload. I didn't take those stickers because
I wanted them, I took them because I wanted to be noticed, I
wanted to be thought of – I was acting out. She knew that as she
held me tight, and she wanted me to know it, too – that I wasn't
a bad person, I'd just done a bad thing. That single moment of
compassion and empathy overwhelmed me then, as it does now
recalling it. To know I was loved and that I was able to talk to
someone and ultimately be understood probably changed my
life forever.

Doing the podcast has cemented that feeling about my Nanny
Queenie, and when I see guests get emotional about their own

mentors, it just reinforces how much these mentors change our lives, and that it's the little moments that often have the biggest impact.

So, to all the mentors out there, this is for you – from the very bottom of my heart. Thank you x.

JIM

It's amazing how many blank moments the education system throws up for young people (and their parents). From an early age, there is pressure to do well and pick the right school. Then there are GCSEs, and the need to start narrowing things down and picking the subjects that will lead into your working career. It's a ridiculously young age to put pressure on kids to make big life decisions. Most of the adults I know (including this one, massively!) didn't know what they really wanted to do until they were much older. Some still don't! And that's totally fine. Life is about exploring the world, and discovering things about yourself as you go. I actually really love it when someone I know announces they are ditching the suit and tie in order to go travelling, or become a snorkel instructor, or go back to university; or even the other way round, when they say they're ditching the freelance life because they've decided to go into a 'proper career'. Making switches like that when you're a 'grown-up' takes balls, and I respect it enormously.

I change my career roughly every two years or so. I don't think I've lasted longer than about 18 months in a full-time position, and that was when I was in my mid-twenties, before I decided to go travelling and move to America to become a soccer coach, which was one of the best decisions I ever made.

Making bold decisions like that came up when we talked to Chris Addison, who – now in his late forties and having been

in the entertainment industry for a quarter of a century –
recounted a conversation with some old friends that made him
look back over his own life decisions. An incredibly successful
comedian, actor and director, Chris knows well the transient
lifestyle of a freelance performer, and admitted he still worries
about money and the future from time to time. But he put it in
the context of some, in his words, 'slightly sad' conversations
he'd recently had with old friends who all had pretty well-
established careers in the civil service or finance, that sort of
thing. What some would describe as 'real jobs'.

What struck Chris was that so many of them were lamenting
that they wished they'd taken more of a risk with their
careers. But now, with mortgages and families, it was basically
impossible to make that leap. Many felt they'd gone as far as
they were going to in terms of career progression, and could
either spend the next ten years trying to make partner (or
whatever people in real jobs do) or just coast and spend time
with their family. In reply, Chris told them that he never feels
secure and work could dry up at any second – but what he said
to us was, deep down, he'd felt relief. Relief that he had done
the thing he chose to do – and had done okay at it. He added
that not everybody gets to do that; not everybody makes that
decision and sees it go well.

I was nodding the whole way through when Chris was talking.
(Except the bit about those life decisions leading to success –
that is, hopefully, still to come for me.) But that feeling of relief
at having chosen the path he wanted to take, rather than the
one he felt he should, resonated hugely with me. I was a fairly
average kid academically, I guess; not massively into school, but
I didn't struggle. I was more concerned with playing football on
the playground and swapping Panini Premier League stickers.

At secondary school, I treated most of those academic subjects
like housework: not fun on any level, but they had to be done

and I was okay at them. I didn't mind the more creative subjects like art, but I still had no real desire to do anything more than go home and play football in the park until the sun went down. I now look back and realise that when my mum told me countless times to maybe concentrate on something other than football, she may have had a point.

It was sheer luck – and probably mostly genetics – that saw me leave school with 11 GSCEs (mostly Cs, a couple of Bs, and, weirdly, an A in French chucked in). Still only really caring about football, I went to a different school for sixth form and did the aforementioned PE (failed in first year), Ceramics (also failed in first year due to the coursework, despite having a love of making things), General Studies (meh), French (scraped by) and Communication Studies (found I loved it, to my surprise). Generally, my two years doing A-Levels were miserable, and I spent most of my time avoiding school, aided by the girls in my French class who (as I was the only boy) took me under their wing. They facilitated me skipping school because they were all so good and could have passed without going to any lessons, which we all often didn't. Funny and entertaining friends they were, but in many ways, they weren't great influences. That said, I would have found a way not to go to those French classes even without their influence.

There was a flicker of hope, like a lone candle in a dark room, in Communication Studies (where the Palace fanzine I talked about in Chapter 7 was born). During my 'gap year', when most kids were off travelling to fantastic places like Goa and Brazil, I went to the rather less salubrious Tonbridge in Kent to retake my French A-Level and do the full Media Studies A-Level in one year. I walked away with an A in Media Studies and got my French up to a D, which was enough to go to university. It really was only at that point that I realised I liked writing creatively and decided, tentatively, to do a journalism degree and see where it went.

But even then, I spent those three years not really knowing what I wanted to do, deciding early on I didn't want to be a reporter as it felt like too much work, and still trying to play football as much as possible – including semi-professionally for Fareham Town (reserves), down the road from uni in Southampton. It was only after university, when I was doing work experience at my local newspaper back home in Kent, that I decided I wanted to be a football reporter – and to be honest, I probably would have done that regardless of getting a degree. Going to university just felt, for me, like something I was supposed to do, and apart from making some incredible friends, learning how (not) to deal with money and playing many, many, many hours of Football Manager, I didn't do much else.

In fact, this will tell you how much it was worth it: I finished my third year with a 2:2 in Journalism. I did a terrible thesis which, for some reason, I decided to write about Trevor McDonald and to this day I'm still not sure why. I think, looking back, I wasn't brilliantly guided; that's to say, I did the thesis without even trying to interview Trevor, which should have been the first port of call. I had no idea what I was doing with my coursework, to be honest. But I will say that the social side of going to university really helped me to grow. I may have come away with a degree that wasn't really worth the paper it was written on – and, knowing me, probably full of typos – but I did grow up mentally during my three years there and if that's what I was supposed to get out of going to university, then it was worth it.

So I then spent almost a year trying to get an entry-level job in local journalism, but when I asked my course leader from uni to write a recommendation for me, he wrote: 'James was a willing student who qualified with a strong 2:1,' which was clearly a typo but I thought, 'Well, he's written it so let's just go along with it.' To this day, no one has ever checked, and I worked for almost a decade in national journalism until I started doing comedy full-time.

When I did that week's work experience on the sports desk of the *Kent and Sussex Courier*, I loved interviewing local footballers and decided I wanted to be a football writer. I got my first job after meeting the sports editor of my local newspaper while we both did weekend shifts subediting at the *Independent on Sunday* – which I only got because the weekend editor was the son-in-law of my mum and dad's neighbour. A job came up as news reporter on the Uckfield patch (RIP), and the only qualification they were interested in was not a degree, but the NCTJ prelims. Even though my degree course offered them, I hadn't done them, as it was extra work and I'd been convinced I didn't want to be a reporter three years previously. But I got the job on the back of the sports editor's recommendation.

Remember how I mentioned it's not what you know but who you know?

Chris Addison hit the nail on the head again when he said that, when it comes to education in the UK, we are so used to narrowing down our options that we often don't see that there are other sides to us that we should at least be exploring. He added that there is something quite terrifying about the idea of cutting opportunities off. I appreciate that it's impossible for kids to study every subject, but I certainly felt that I had to start making career decisions from a very young age and pick what I wanted to do when really, I had no idea – and still didn't, for many years after.

What I've learned from my own career, and certainly from talking to the wide range of creative guests on our podcast, is that life is full of twists and turns and it's okay to change your mind. And although I have only just moaned about uni not quite being the experience I thought it was going to be, I'm still glad I went, as I grew a lot during that time. I learned things I didn't realise I'd learned until many years later. And I still love Trevor McDonald.

BLANK

The most important thing I've discovered in my subsequent years as a 'professional' whatever-it-is-I-do is that it's you who has the final say. You can do a job you hate for years, or you can decide to leave it and try something else. It's your call. I'm glad I have been true to myself and chosen what I've wanted to do at every turn, even though I am nowhere near as successful as Chris Addison. Although, of course, success is all relative. I am happy, well-off enough only to worry about income every other month, and I have done and seen some amazing things during my varied work life. When I got back from coaching soccer in America in 2009, I took a temping job in an insurance firm, just to make ends meet. I only lasted two weeks, as I hated it so much. I vowed then to do what I wanted professionally, no matter how badly I would be paid – and I'm still here today doing precisely that, and still getting badly paid. I don't have a massive house or a fancy car or take many holidays (if any). But I'm doing what makes me happy. Though I had many blank moments at school – blank exam pages and blank spaces on my attendance record – I guess all those subjects I disliked did at least push me towards knowing what I don't like; this in turn pushed me towards making those things I *do* like into my job. If that's what school gave me, then I guess I'm grateful. I just never want to open an exam paper ever again.

———

Comedian Rachel Parris knows what she likes, and a lot of it comes from education – where, unlike a lot of comedians, she thrived.

She told us she liked the formality of education. It worked for her. And that structure is something she uses in her performances today. In comedy, she said, it is unusual for a comedian to have had a positive experience of formal education, because so many comedians would class themselves as anti-establishment. But Rachel is pleased to have found that there are more comedians like her, who are just doing comedy their way – even if that doesn't fit the rebellious comedy 'norm'.

For her, writing an Edinburgh show isn't far from schoolwork, in that the structure required is like writing a really good English essay. Then there is the message you are trying to get across in your work – figuring out your message and expressing it is the basis of a lot of schoolwork. This academic aspect of writing comedy really appealed to Rachel, because it's something she was good at when she was younger.

I think I understand what she was saying here. I'm sure most comedians like the writing side of comedy, and some like the performing more than others. Whenever I refer to something as feeling like schoolwork, it's always in a negative way, and I often find writing reminds me of homework or a school project. Clearly Rachel is able to channel those school days, during which she thrived, in her comedy writing. I sometimes feel guilty that I'm not enjoying writing, and that stems from feeling bad at school if I turned in a crappy assignment or got a poor grade. I felt like I'd let my teacher down, and I guess I now feel like I let myself down if I write something terrible.

But I must have learned something from school: the basics of writing; the fact that a deadline actually helps push me to get something done; the fact that working alongside others is something I enjoy from time to time. It can't have been all that bad because, I did go to some lessons, and despite wanting to just play football all day, every day, I clearly did pick up a few academic traits along the way.

It's funny what we all take away from our education and apply to our careers. I was someone who never really thought I would use anything I'd learned in school in my adult life. Pythagoras's theorum? Pointless. I think I assumed that I would just pick up what I needed along the way, and to be honest I mainly have done; but having listened to our guests talk about their education and experiences of school, I've realised I wasn't the only one who meandered through and did what I could. We all did, with varying degrees of success.

The other benefit of schooling was that you just had to get your head down and work, there was no way round it, and for many comedians and perfomers, that is how they succeed in their careers. Just getting on with it despite everything. One comedian on the podacast – a legend and veteran of the stand-up game – until the COVID-19 lockdown, hadn't had more than a month off gigs in 22 years. That relentless pursuit of just doing what you're supposed to do is pure schoolwork.

I admitted I didn't quite approach comedy in the same way, mostly through a feeling of imposter syndrome, even though I actually would love to be as hard-working. This comedian said it was just the way he'd always done things, which I suspected again was a mentality from school days, but he did also joke that I'm probably not damaged enough as an individual to do comedy. That's probably something for my counsellor to unpack – thanks a lot!

Chapter 10:
Switching Off

All the positive change I have made in my life has involved taking action. You don't think your way into a better way of living – you live your way into a better way of thinking.

Marcus Brigstocke

The idea of switching off in the 21st century is a challenging proposition. As I'm writing this book, I find myself on a browser with approximately 12 tabs open: emails, social media, some random website about quizzes, Spotify, and a bunch of others I can't even remember opening. I know any second now, I will stop writing this and hover over one or more of those tabs and click on it …

I wrote that 45 minutes ago!

There's a wonderful scene in the comedy series *Gavin and Stacey* where a group of characters are travelling from Barry Island to Billericay for a Christmas celebration. They've stopped at a motorway services to have a break, and Dave the coach driver is sitting and playing a racing car arcade machine and proclaiming it's so good to have a break from the driving.

This is a bit like how I see social media and the internet in general: a distraction, yes; a chance to actually switch off, no.

We are always 'on', even in those moments when we don't think we are. There's a constant stream of notifications coming through on our phones and computers, and according to research we check our phones every six minutes – so approximately 120 times in a 12-hour period, which sounds fairly remarkable when you see it in writing.

As we touched on in Chapter 4, the idea that platforms such as Twitter give us a little respite during our working day is a total fallacy. These platforms send our brains into overdrive – for good or bad reasons – and they can be said to make our internal chemicals react.

We first talked on the *Blank Podcast* about the subject of being switched on all the time with screenwriter Warren Dudley, as his experience of missing out on family stuff because of work is something he is only too aware of.

Warren explained how things for him never really start or end, he's just at it all the time. At times, he wishes he had a switch that meant he could turn his work brain off at about 8 p.m. and then turn it back on again in the morning. The moments Warren feels it the most are when he's spending time with his daughter, whom he tries to give his full attention to. But they might watch an entire film together, and afterwards Warren couldn't tell you a single detail about the plot; he admitted that he'll stare at the screen, but is nearly always thinking about his own creative stuff. Lately he's been trying to stop thinking constantly about himself and his projects, scripts and stories, and think instead about how to switch off.

It felt like a brave thing to admit at the time, but it happens to the best of us – life takes over, as a lot of people seem to say these days. Is this perhaps the result of our fast pace of life, particularly in the Western world, where we seem to have lost sight of any sort of downtime? We work increasingly long hours with short breaks, and the nine-to-five model is slowly dissipating with every year.

Our minds are often in a state very much like my browser with the gazillions of tabs open, so how can we go about closing them down so that we can devote our energies to less – and, in turn, increase our productivity, or even actually relax now and then?

SINGLE-TASKING

In 2001 at Michigan State University, researchers created an experiment to see the extent to which distractions would impair students' work. Participants had to perform a sequence of tasks on a computer, but would be interrupted by a pop-up window at various times. These pop-ups required a code to be entered before the participants could return to what they were doing. The interruptions that occurred every 2.8–3 seconds doubled the rate of error on their tasks, and at 4-second intervals, the errors were tripled and, in some cases, quadrupled.

So, why do we multitask? As humans, we often feel fairly elated and pleased with ourselves while we are multitasking – we feel like we are achieving so much when we can watch TV and look at Twitter while also reading emails and checking WhatsApp. We may even feel like multitasking superheroes, but we are rarely doing any of those tasks with genuine conviction or focus – however smug they might make us feel.

Scientifically, it's been shown that our brains are not capable of multitasking at all; in fact, it causes the brain to 'split' as it tries to cope with the various tasks by flitting back and forth between each activity, creating 'spotlights'. It's this switching that takes the highest toll – the brain just can't manage it.

Some researchers had thought our brains would adapt and find new ways to take on more than one thing at a time; however, this has proved not to be the case. In several experiments carried out by Stanford professor Clifford Nass, it was proven that multitasking led participants to be incredibly bad at filtering out irrelevant information, and their performance was severely diminished compared to those attempting to take on a single task. And researchers at the Institute of Psychiatry at the University of London found that multitasking using electronic media actually caused a greater decrease in IQ for employees at a British company than if they had been smoking pot or losing a night's sleep.

BLANK

One simple idea is to have just one tab open in your browser – that way you can truly take on one online task at a time. Another thing to consider is making a to-do list each night for the following day, and ticking them off one by one as you go. This will help you to establish a good routine moving forward.

Taking regular (non-screen!) breaks from a task can help to give the brain a little breather and enable you to refocus again. And above all, unless absolutely necessary, turn your phone off!

Dedicating yourself to a single task will feel strange for some at first, but once you realise how much more productive you can be, it will feel revolutionary – and also give your poor brain the break it so richly deserves! It's pretty obvious when you actually think about it: we should never bite off more than we can chew.

And Clifford Nass has some good news for those, like me, who like to listen to music while they work: 'In the case of music, it's a little different. We have a special part of our brain for music, so we can listen to music while we do other things.'

Phew!

———

Sometimes we find that work takes over and the idea of taking time out from what you do – especially when what you do is such a huge part of who you are – seems next to impossible. It was something we discussed with comedian and actor Rufus Hound, whose theatre work means he often misses out on big occasions. As Rufus told us, live performance – or as he called it, 'showing off' – usually happens when other people aren't at work, and so he is off working when everyone else is around and doing non-work things.

So when people invite Rufus to their birthday parties, wedding anniversaries, bar mitzvahs, engagement parties, gender reveal events – whatever the occasion is – he's often not going to be there because he'll be at work. It's a bit of a strange situation, because rather than being in a place where he's surrounded by affection and love as he celebrates the meaningful moments of the people he loves and respects, he's instead somewhere else, trying to win the approval of strangers.

I totally empathised with Rufus here, having spent too long at the computer writing or with my head in the clouds – or, like Warren, constantly dreaming up ideas and projects and not being present in the moment with those I care about. It's something I am trying to work on, and I've realised that the concept of single-tasking could benefit my personal life, too. It would give those around me dedicated time and focus – rather than having to deal with a multitasking Giles who isn't ever fully there.

BLANK

JIM

I think it's hard for any creative person to completely switch off. We've heard how a lot of creative people have trouble sleeping because their brain is constantly whirring away, and how the best ideas can come out of the blue when you are doing something mundane like washing up or having a shower. Choosing a career in writing or performing means you are very rarely off the clock.

Someone who does a 'real job', to quote Chris Addison, might be able to leave the office, close their briefcase (do people still use briefcases?), get on the train or in the car, go home and forget about their work. They can have a nice dinner with their family, read bedtime stories to their kids, and settle down on the sofa with a nice glass of wine to enjoy their favourite Netflix show with their partner. Man, that sounds amazing – why didn't I choose that life?!

If you're doing a 'normal' job that maybe isn't particularly stimulating, you may find yourself staring out the window daydreaming, and your boss will probably tell you off for switching off during work hours. But for me and many other creatives, daydreaming is an important part of what we do.

I absolutely loved the TV show *Scrubs* and I related so hard to main character Dr John Dorian (known fondly by everyone as 'J.D.'). So much so that, after I started watching it and realised I also have those initials, I started insisting everyone refer to me as J.D. – something that has stuck to this day. There was also his haphazardness, his sweet but naive approach to life, and his obsession with his hair – traits I shared big-time.

J.D. has a knack for slipping into intense daydreams, usually imagining some wacky escapade in the form of a cutaway or some memory from his ever-increasing pool of embarrassing moments (something else we both share). Although, as we're about to discover, J.D. might actually have a psychiatric condition – which, let's face it, he probably should know about, being a doctor and all.

During our podcast with Fiona Murden, she mentioned that we spend, on average, 50 per cent of our time daydreaming. She said that could include mind-wandering, reflecting and planning – they all count. In fact, as I've been writing this chapter and have started to think about how daydreaming affects the brain and has an impact on creativity, I've found that it's taking me twice as long as it should – because I've been daydreaming about daydreaming. It's an incredibly powerful distraction – so powerful, in fact, that it can actually take over some people's lives ...

I daydream a lot, but I normally just drift off into a different world for five or ten minutes before snapping out of it pretty quickly and thinking nothing else of it. But for some people, daydreaming isn't just something that distracts them for a minute or two while at work or while going about mundane daily tasks; it's actually a condition called maladaptive daydreaming (MD), and it is *intense.*

Identified by Professor Eli Somer of the University of Haifa in Israel in 2002, and as yet not officially classified as a disorder or with any official treatment, the causes and effects of maladaptive daydreaming are still being researched. Doing so is like opening a door onto a whole new world.

Jayne Bigelsen wrote about her experiences with the condition in *The Atlantic* in 2015, and it sounds like a lot.* Whereas the average person might daydream for a bit about a friend or a situation or a material object, Jayne will imagine whole movie-like scenarios and fully developed characters, with herself immersed in the plot. During school and then university, she would find excuses to escape her mundane day-to-day existence and delve back into her internal world, including asking intentionally complicated questions in class so that the teacher would take a while to explain the answer (leaving her time and space to daydream).

Her immersive daydreaming began to take over her life, and she would revisit the same characters and situations – often living out full-length episodes, complete with cliffhangers for next week. To put a positive spin on it, she is clearly a very, very creative person, but she found that this amount of creativity was getting in the way of her life. She had been struggling with these intense, vivid, all-consuming daydreams since she was a

BLANK

---

* https://www.theatlantic.com/health/archive/2015/04/when-daydreaming-replaces-real-life/391319/.

child, and it took a lifetime of research on her part to find out that a) it was even a thing, and b) that there were other people who were suffering from it. As a 12-year-old in the late 1990s, it had left her feeling pretty alone, but there are now online support groups, like the Wild Minds Network, with thousands of people sharing their experiences and giving each other advice – and, at times, working on understanding this condition at a rate so fast, science can't always keep up.

People who visit the forum report losing their jobs, struggling to have successful relationships, or even avoiding human contact altogether in order to concentrate on their daydreams. Some even contemplate suicide. The fact it has taken so long for maladaptive daydreaming to be something that people talk about shows how many in the medical industry were quick to write these symptoms off. Even now, the average person can often underestimate just how powerful our brains are. I know I do. We take for granted the multitude of sums they do each day, or the thousands of cognitive commands they send around our bodies. So when they start going into overdrive and making us experience almost virtual realities, we might not appreciate that, for some people, it can be a debilitating condition.

Jayne offered herself as case study as a way to understand MD better, and an MRI scan showed that the same part of the brain that lights up when an alcoholic sees a bottle of whisky also shifts into gear when a maladaptive daydreamer starts daydreaming. Daydreaming had become a drug to Jayne, and her addiction was only getting stronger and stronger. And yet I don't think this is something to be feared, and that is a conclusion Jayne also lands on in her writing.

In 2010, Roger Freeman, a researcher at the University of British Columbia, published a journal article titled 'Stereotypic Movement Disorder: Easily Missed', focusing on 42 children whose parents or teachers had expressed concern about their unusual repetitive motions. When the kids were asked what was happening, 83 per cent said they were repeating stories in their heads. The initial reaction from medical professionals was to try to find a way to solve it, but the children reported enjoying the stories, and Freeman looked at it more philosophically. 'Many of the children were already creative,' he noted. 'Do we want to stamp out creativity or not?'

I tell you about Jayne and J.D. not to scare you, but to help you understand that the brain is an organ to be respected. We've already heard from Fiona about how we need to look after it by getting more sleep, because otherwise it can break down or go into overdrive. Our brains are both the best thing about us and the worst – they need to be treated like family heirlooms, because in many ways they are. After learning about maladaptive daydreaming and talking to Fiona on the podcast, I've certainly realised that I need to look after my brain more. The idea of maladaptive daydreaming – that the brain can be that powerful – is scary. It's a reminder that we have been given a very powerful tool, but like laptops, if they break down, we lose everything. If I look after my brain better, then it will look after me.

But how do we actually get our brains to stop whirring away when we need a break? How do we *actually* switch off? When we had Fiona on the podcast, we didn't want to pass up the opportunity to find out more about how we can treat our brains better.

Our brains are so busy and our lives are so chaotic that trying to give ourselves a chance to restore to factory settings is really important, Fiona said. And one way in which we can do this is mindfulness.

BLANK

Mindfulness is the practice of connecting with what you are sensing and feeling in the current moment, and not getting distracted by your thoughts or concerns about the past or future. We do this mainly through meditation. Fiona is a big fan of mindfulness and added that we, as people – and this is true even of psychologists – are not really taught how to work with our minds effectively. She said she was surprised to realise how little she knew, despite all her training, and that the more you know, the more you don't know.

I have to admit I don't practise mindfulness. I absolutely love the idea of it, and what Fiona said all made sense to me, but I've always been someone who says, 'Yeah, it's great, but I don't have the time for it,' even though the time needed is literally a few minutes. There's something about taking myself out of whatever I am engrossed in – even if it's pointless things like Twitter or Facebook – that makes me feel like I am missing out. Which, of course, I'm not – but I have constant FOMO. Fiona explained that mindfulness is like exercise for our brains. It connects parts of the brain that need to be connected for us to function properly, and by not doing it, I am basically asking my brain to function without the necessary training. It's like trying to play in the World Cup final having not kicked a ball for a year.

When we interviewed TV comedy legend John Lloyd, he spoke about how mindfulness had helped him. He talked about meditating as being a positive example of blankness, and how it is about trying to get to the point where you are not thinking, but are conscious. Imagine driving down a motorway you know well, and it's like you suddenly wake up and you're at exit 24 already – your body is doing the driving without you really being aware of it, and so you are conscious, but not thinking about what you are doing.

John told us the story of Martha Reeves, a nun who, for a number of years, moved each summer to the Alaskan coast, where she caught her own fish and lived in solitude. She spent her winters in Oxford, working on illuminated medieval manuscripts. An incredible person, he said. As she told John, she believes in silence (as indicated by her book, *Silence: A User's Guide* written under the name Maggie Ross) and that accessing the stillness at the heart of a person is precious.

As Fiona said, most of the mind is full of needless chatter, just a monkey in your head, yapping away, going over the past, dwelling on shame and embarrassment, and worrying about the future. The brain, John told us, is more complicated than the US economy, and there are more cells in the brain than there are trees in the Amazon rainforest. The number of connections the brain makes in a day is a number so huge it cannot be written down – and what are we using it for? Mostly nonsense.

John then got out his mobile phone and talked about his 'Inverse Law of Technology', which states that the more sophisticated the communication device, the more banal the information transferred on it is. People sharing pictures of their eggs for breakfast, he said, on a mobile phone capable of doing incredible, wondrous, important things.

The brain is the same. It can write incredible symphonies and plays and create any number of other amazing things, but this creativity is blocked by mundane gunge. All that chatter is there to keep us stupid, John added, but meditation clears all that out and gets you back to the important stuff: being alive, breathing. He added he was sceptical about it at first, but realised it was a holiday for the mind and massively helpful, especially in getting the mind ready to be creative.

The brain is like any other muscle – you have to exercise it. Fiona explained that meditation strengthens the neural connections between the frontal lobe of the brain and our emotional sensors, which makes it easier for us to manage our emotions. If we can strengthen those connections, it allows us to keep the more primitive part of the brain in check. Fiona admitted that, even as psychologist, she doesn't treat her brain properly or give it the care it needs. She added that everything is a fine line. Mental health is a fine line. Whether you are someone who is narcissistic or merely confident is a fine line. Whether you have imposter syndrome or you are just under-confident is a fine line.

When I hear the expression 'fine line', I often think of someone balancing on a tripwire above a ravine, or between two tall buildings like Philippe Petit in the 2008 documentary *Man on Wire*. And that's how I see mental health a lot of the time: you're up there, carrying all your baggage, and trying to get from one side to the other without falling off that thin wire into the pit of despair, with no safety net to catch you. It's interesting to hear a trained psychologist say basically the same – that there are fine lines between personality traits and mental states. It's made me appreciate something I think I already knew: that the brain is a delicate machine.

We are trying to pour so much information into our brains, and to get them to print out creative scripts or prize-winning novels or whatever we are trying to produce, but if the machine itself is broken, then we'll never be able to print anything out.

I don't think I've ever really looked after my brain, and I'm starting to realise I've had many problems with creativity and mental health as a result. It all starts, and ends, with the wiring of our brains. And if we can manage to truly switch off from time to time, our brains will function better, and we can create better things and be better people.

Chapter 11:
The Power of
Conversation

Alan Alda, who is one of the most inspiring people I've ever met and is also a really good friend, once said, 'The reason why you hear people out, they could be wrong about absolutely everything, except the one thing that is going to change your life, and that's why you hear them out.'

Sanjeev Bhaskar

Conversation, for me, is the time when you and others are thinking together, finding common ground, discovering differences and putting meaning into one another's lives.

Before we started the podcast, I'd lost my way in terms of communicating with new people, making sure I stayed safe in my own personal echo chamber and inner circle. Wanting to reach out and change that was part of this podcast's conception: to have new conversations with new people; to move beyond my echo chamber; and hopefully to figure out some tactics to avoid the blank moments that were continually occurring in my life at that time.

I won't suggest that I am in any way a conversationalist. I greatly admire people who have pushed the podcast boundaries in recent years – people like Marc Maron, Joe Rogan, Adam Buxton – and I love podcasts like *The Receipts*, *The High Low* with Dolly Alderton and Pandora Sykes, and *The Scummy Mummies*, where conversation (rather than interviewing) is king. That's what Jim and I wanted to do from the off – chat rather than interview people, and be facilitators for conversation rather than having a set plan.

What was obvious within a few episodes was how powerful conversation can truly be, how liberating and inspiring sharing thoughts and ideas is for us, and how connecting with others is not only stimulating but life-affirming. We'd discovered our own form of therapy, our own form of education, our very own think tank in which we were collecting invaluable data.

We are social creatures and being social is good for us. There is even research to show that lengthier chats are far more beneficial than shooting the breeze for a couple of minutes.

Professor Matthias Mehl and his team at the University of Arizona performed a study on the link between well-being and conversation. The study showed that participants who had longer, more in-depth conversations and discussions were happier overall than those who only spoke with others for a short period of time. Professor Mehl noted: 'In substantive conversation, there is real, meaningful information exchanged. Importantly, it could be about any topic – politics, relationships, the weather – it just needs to be at a more than trivial level of depth.' And it makes total sense when you think about it: we establish a far greater connection and build more trust when we talk about things that go beyond surface level. I'd even go as far as to say that deeper conversation can be exhilarating at times.

Where the *Blank Podcast* is concerned, the deeper connection formed over the hour or more we often have with our guests allows us to really get to know how they tick; and it also enables us to discover organically what their own blank moments have been. Discussing these difficult times in their lives is something that benefits all of us – the guests, us as hosts, and of course our listeners.

At the end of each episode, as a sort of summary of our conversation, we ask our guests to give some advice on dealing with blank moments. And, as will have become clear by reading this book, 'blank' means something different to everyone, and can be very subjective.

So in this chapter, we'll share a few of our very favourite tips and strategies to help anyone with their blank moments – indeed, we have attempted many of them ourselves ...

What I do is I visualise a favourite place ... there's a long mountain walk in the western Highlands near where we go. It's a part of the world I very much adore; I find it spiritually overwhelming. I'm not a spiritual person, but I find that there's something just greater than the sum of the parts, something transcendent about it, and there's a 4-mile walk through a forest where I go with Maxwell and we get to the bottom of a mountain called Beinn Sgritheall ... and there's no one else around for miles and there's a little lochan – a lochan is a tiny little loch – and the stream burbling into it. [I sit on] the stone there, which is almost like a natural seat ... and all I can hear is the water and the wind and the birds and that is it. And so I think of myself in that situation and all of a sudden I feel calm, and I'm feeling much calmer now.

Nicky Campbell

When thoughts are in our heads [they] swim around, and it's a bit like putting dye into a swimming pool – it's like that dye will just spread, and you can't really see where the original drop was that you put in. Whereas if you write it down, it slows your brain down, for a start – and it means that you're processing it, because you're making sense of it as you're writing it down. So it's similar to saying it out loud, it's putting a structure around it, and it's going through a process of putting it in order in your brain as you put it down on paper. And that can be even if you're free-writing. Sometimes as you're writing creatively, you get blank moments and you get blocked, and one of the things people say is to just write anything.

Fiona Murden

Early etymology says [the word 'blank'] is an absence of colour. That implies that 'blank' is always something negative, but it doesn't have to be; a blank piece of paper has endless possibilities.

Susie Dent

This idea that out of blankness we can create something is an extremely comforting notion. This book started off as a blank page, and many, many pages later, we have created something from nothing.

Being in the right environment is always a good way of getting through blank moments in creativity. Reginald D. Hunter is fully aware of how much of a difference this makes to his process:

> I find for myself, I look at my career process, I cannot summon the information from the universe – but what I can do is create an environment where it's conducive for it to come. So I can make sure my house is quiet or I've got the music that I need, smoke the thing I need to – whatever you need to do to make the thing come, you can do that. And what I find when I'm blocked or blank, there is something else going on in my life that is blocking me or making me blank, and usually when I get blocked, I'm being dishonest with myself about something in some way. It's like the universe looks at me and says, 'So, we're bullshitting ourselves this week, so this means we don't want any new jokes for a while.'

When we spoke to actress and screenwriter Rachel Shenton, she told us her own feelings of going blank came after finishing her Oscar-winning short film *The Silent Child*:

> I remember when the film was finished, thinking, 'Now what? We've done that.' Because the whole way through you're wanting to finish it, you're wanting to make that movie and watch it and be happy with it, and then it was 'And now what?'

That 'what next?' feeling often happens to me after a long project, especially one I've put my heart and soul into, but it comes back to what Susie Dent said – that sometimes embracing the blank moment and seeing it as a canvas waiting to be painted on is an exciting possibility.

When author Lindsay Galvin spoke about her blank moments, she said that when she is not in a good place mentally, it often affects her doing her best work:

> The good stuff sometimes comes out of the angst and pain of the process, but I don't believe you have to be tortured to be creative. I don't like to hear about how sloping around feeling miserable is when the best work comes; my best work definitely doesn't come when I'm feeling like that.

Presenter Julia Bradbury had a good idea that could certainly help in those times when you're not quite at the races:

> My one bit of advice, if you're put on the spot and can't answer the question, is to buy yourself time – and you can do that in a variety of ways: you can bounce back another question. Delay your answer by saying something like, 'let me answer that in a moment,' or reassemble the question with the phrase, 'I can't answer that until we focus on ...' Really just do your research, and if you've done your homework – even if you only know part of the answer – it's something you can fall back on.

I love this idea about giving yourself time, especially when it comes to those difficult situations or blank moments. We are often so quick to try to resolve, repair or keep going, but actually taking some time out to breathe and take stock of things is really beneficial.

But our compulsion to keep on keeping on during even the blankest of times is something Mark Gatiss talked about with us – that by continuing to work, we might bypass the blank moments:

I'm just reading this wonderful biography of Bram Stoker, and he was astonishingly hard-working. I think he basically worked himself to death, but it's almost difficult to understand how he did it [all] – he was working on a newspaper in Dublin, writing around ten reviews a week, sometimes he'd re-review a show, and he had a full-time civil service job, and he must have been writing at work. How did he do all this stuff? But I think sometimes people have a passion ... he was desperate to work, and desperate to work in the theatre and not be a civil servant.

A lot of advice we've received from our guests on the podcast has centred around the idea of acceptance – that when all is said and done, blank moments will occur whether we like it or not, and that by accepting them, we can figure out how to move forward. Even if, as Rachel Parris described, you are someone who is very organised:

I think for writing, I think accepting that there are days when it's not going to work for you, even if I've already said to you, or I've put in my diary, 'Today is a day to write,' and I think it's good to try on that day, but it's good to accept that when you can't do it. And then I think the times or the hour that gets you on that road – really go with it, if you can afford to, whether that's just for half an hour or whether that's for a day, give as much time as you can. It's a bit like a rolling ball – once you're on that road, more stuff will come and you can make the most of that.

Cartoonist Mike Dicks takes on blank moments by breaking things down:

For any problem that you get, break it down into smaller bits and do one of the smaller bits. So if I get a blank moment, I try to apply some form of process which means I can do something towards the ultimate aim that isn't actually the ultimate thing.

I really like this way of breaking things down, and it's something I have definitely applied during the process of writing this book. Working on the bigger themes within it has been made easier by listening back to sections of the transcripts to make sure the subjects are fully examined.

We often think we are alone in our blank moments, that we've got to figure this stuff out by ourselves. Actress and writer Jess Impiazzi told us that she deals with her own blank times through 'ikigai', a term that means 'a reason for being':

> We get stuck sometimes, because you might get told by your parents, friends or family members that the thing you want to do is an impossible dream, just because perhaps they couldn't do it or rather they could do it but chose not to. And one thing I always say is, if you don't believe in yourself, then no one else is going to.

Dame Kelly Holmes shared with us her own unique method, by talking about going within to dig her way out and reassure herself during a time of blankness:

> Find those moments where you were who you wanted to be – the driver or the vision or your motivator for your goal. Remember those things when it's going horribly wrong and then maybe from that re-evaluate and figure out how to bring those things back into play. Don't think that that blank moment is the end.

Whatever your own blanks might be, we hope this book may have given you some moments of empathy, and some insights and takeaways that might help you in your own journey through life – whether you're a creative or a sportsperson or even the

next prime minister. Because some things in life are universal,
and while we may all deal with them differently, the knowledge
that we are connected by the difficulties we face can sometimes
be a very comforting thing.

Everyone is creative, and our biggest asset and our biggest liability is our creativity – because we can, when we're down, convince ourselves that we are the worst thing that ever existed, that we are pointless and shit at everything. And the flip side is you can think you are the best thing since sliced bread, and you know everything – and that is just us, that's our brains.

Sanjeev Bhaskar

Epilogue:
Next Steps

So, moving forward, what can you do to help you to avoid blank moments, to reflect on the good things and positive things you have in your life, and to soothe you when things do – inevitably – just go wrong?

GRATITUDE LIST

When we had comedian Marcus Brigstocke on as a guest, he spoke about his time recovering from addiction and told us about an exercise that he has taken from that time in his life. Every morning, he writes a 'gratitude list'.

A gratitude list is a written list of things for which a person is grateful and it's used to help identify and focus on the positive things in one's life. Marcus shares his daily gratitude list with friends and family. It has been an important part of his recovery, but for him, it's also a chance to see all the things in his life that mean the most to him written down.

We thought this was such a powerful thing and something to do ourselves, so here are a few ideas to get you started with your own gratitude list:

- Make it personal to you. You don't necessarily need a fancy journal or a special pen, it could just be on your phone, but make sure it's something that you personally connect with.

- There aren't any rules for making a gratitude list – it's yours – so don't set yourself any particular goals if you don't want to. The key is not to get stressed about it, and to give yourself the time and space to do it.

- Keep it short and simple. You don't need to write an essay.

- Make it part of your daily routine, and set an alarm if you think you might forget. Doing it regularly will eventually lead to it becoming a habit.

- Try doing it in the morning to set you up for the day.

- Some days will be easier than others – don't beat yourself up if you can't think of anything to write down.

- A gratitude list really is a simple and effective way to give yourself a little bit of perspective, practise some self-care and feel some happiness each day, so please do give it a go yourself. It can be a truly beautiful thing.

In hosting the podcast and writing this book, it's struck us how much meaningful advice our guests have given us – sometimes without even realising it – and how interpreting this advice and putting it into practice has become known to us as 'blankfulness'.

This simple but sage list is specifically designed to help soothe anyone who might be having their own difficult moment. It includes ideas and steps you can adopt at any time to help you regroup and reset.

1. Practise self-compassion.

2. Lean in – when gently turning towards pain, people report that they experience less of it, and their resistance usually decreases.

3. Create a positive mantra for yourself and use it regularly.

4. Visualise your happy place.

5. Create a gratitude group on WhatsApp and share your thoughts.

6. Meditate.

7. Reach out to friends and family you haven't seen in a while.

8. Take a vacation from social media.

9. Break whatever is making you have a blank moment into smaller, more manageable chunks.

10. Say whatever is blanking you out loud, even if no one is there – *especially* if no one is there.

11. Journal! Write down whatever is worrying you or holding you back, even if you never read it again.

12. Breathe!

13. Do some Lego or a jigsaw puzzle – immerse yourself in it and turn your brain off from everything else.

14. Write a *feasible* to-do list at the start of the day.

15. Remind yourself that nothing is ever wasted.

Potential

Pause

Calm

Review

Opportunity

Creativity

Rest

Blank

Peace

Learning

Mindfulness

Self-care

Reboot

Inspiration

Breath

Resources

If you are suffering from your own blank moments and would like some advice, help or reassurance on any of the themes in this book, please take a look at these resources.

PUBLIC FAILURE

'Everyone Fails. Here's How to Pick Yourself Back Up' by Rachel Simmons. *New York Times.*

www.nytimes.com/guides/working-womans-handbook/how-to-overcome-failure

TED playlist: The Benefits of Failure.

www.ted.com/playlists/the_benefits_of_failure

IMPOSTER SYNDROME

'Feel like a fraud?' by Kirsten Weir. American Psychological Association.

www.apa.org/gradpsych/2013/11/fraud

'Dealing With Impostor Syndrome When You're Treated as an Impostor' by Kristen Wong. *New York Times.*

www.nytimes.com/2018/06/12/smarter-living/dealing-with-impostor-syndrome-when-youre-treated-as-an-impostor.html

TED playlist: Fighting Impostor Syndrome.

www.ted.com/playlists/503/fighting_impostor_syndrome

Lisa and Richard Orbe-Austin

Lisa and Richard have given talks together about imposter syndrome and share information and resources on their Instagram pages: @drorbeaustin and @drrichorbeaustin

GRIEF

'Grief after bereavement or loss', NHS website.

www.nhs.uk/conditions/stress-anxiety-depression/coping-with-bereavement

'Coping with grief', Cruse Bereavement Care charity website.

www.cruse.org.uk/get-help/coping-grief

'Grief and loss support', Health Navigator New Zealand website.

www.healthnavigator.org.nz/support/g/grief-loss

DEALING WITH SOCIAL MEDIA

'How to be more mindful', Mental Health Foundation of New Zealand website (includes a section on mindful ways to use social media).

www.mentalhealth.org.nz/home/our-work/page/21/2/how-to-be-more-mindful

SLEEP

National Sleep Foundation: Sleep Diary (a PDF to help you keep track of your sleep hygiene).

www.sleepfoundation.org/sites/default/files/inline-files/SleepDiaryv6.pdf

css-scs.ca/resources/podcasts

'Sleep Deprivation', The Sleep Council.

sleepcouncil.org.uk/advice-support/sleep-hub/sleep-matters/
sleep-deprivation

SOCIAL ANXIETY

'Social anxiety', NHS website.

www.nhs.uk/conditions/social-anxiety

'Self-help Strategies for Social Anxiety', Anxiety Canada.

www.anxietycanada.com/sites/default/files/adult_hmsocial.pdf

'Social Anxiety', Centre for Clinical Interventions, Australia.

www.cci.health.wa.gov.au/Resources/Looking-After-Yourself/
Social-Anxiety

PARENTING

'Being a Parent When You Have Anxiety', by Vanna Winters.
National Alliance on Mental Illness.

www.nami.org/Blogs/NAMI-Blog/February-2019/Being-a-
Parent-When-You-Have-Anxiety

Twins Trust (listening service for parents of twins, triplets
and more).

twinstrust.org/let-us-help/support/twinline.html

Maternal Mental Health Alliance

maternalmentalhealthalliance.org

Channel Mum
https://www.channelmum.com/

Parent Club (support for Scottish parents).
www.parentclub.scot

Dads Matter UK
www.dadsmatteruk.org

Best Beginnings Baby Buddy app (endorsed by NHS).
www.bestbeginnings.org.uk/baby-buddy

NCT (New parents support).
nct.org.uk; Instagram: @nctcharity

DEPRESSION

'Depression information and support', Mental Health America.
screening.mhanational.org/depression

'Depression: personal blogs and stories', Time to Change.
www.time-to-change.org.uk/category/blog/depression

Creatives Against Depression
www.creativesagainstdepression.com/blog

REDUNDANCY AND WORKPLACE ISSUES

'Coping with redundancy during the pandemic', Mind.
www.mind.org.uk/workplace/coronavirus-and-work/coping-with-redundancy

'Mental health at work', Mind.
www.mind.org.uk/workplace/mental-health-at-work

'Coping with redundancy', NI Direct.
www.nidirect.gov.uk/articles/coping-redundancy

'Five Ways to Wellbeing at Work Toolkit', Mental Health
Foundation of New Zealand.
www.mentalhealth.org.nz/home/our-work/category/42/five-
ways-to-wellbeing-at-work-toolkit

MENTAL HEALTH

Canadian Mental Health Association blog
cmha.ca/blogs

Headspace
www.headspace.com

Mental Health America
screening.mhanational.org/connect

Mental Health Australia
www.mhaustralia.org; Instagram: @aumentalhealth

Mind
www.mind.org.uk; Instagram: @mindcharity

Lorraine Pascale
www.lorrainepascale; Instagram @lorrainepascale

MISCELLANEOUS

www.donothingfor2minutes.com

Acknowledgements

JIM

We have so many people to thank for making this book come together, so here goes:

To Céline Hughes and the wonderful team at Quadrille for believing in our vision of turning the podcast into a book, and for guiding us through every step.

To Sam, Lizzy, John and the team at Acast for giving us the platform to make the podcast a possibility, for the studio space and excellent snacks available in the kitchen. Thank you also to the team at Nordic Bar on Newman Street in London for being so accommodating many, many times and letting us record there, as well as Frequency café in Kings Cross for the recording space and lovely hot chocolates.

To Becky Bagnell at Lindsay Literary Agency, for guiding me through my first attempt at writing a book and being brilliant.

To every single guest that has appeared on the podcast (many of whom aren't featured in this book), who have all been incredibly friendly, open and just super lovely to chat to. Special mention to those featured in the book for agreeing to be included. We really appreciate it.

A massive thank you to anyone who has listened to the *Blank Podcast*, whether it's to one episode or all of them – we cannot thank you enough for your support, and if you have tweeted us a nice message or left an iTunes review or sent us an email or just recommended it to a friend, you've helped us more than you'll ever know. And to anyone who has now bought this book, thank you! I never imagined I'd be an author, so the fact you have decided this book is for you has made my year.

To my wife, Miranda, for stopping me throwing my laptop out of the window many, many times, and our daughter, Maria, who keeps us on our toes and has brought us so much joy in a year already. To my mother-in-law Linda, for the support, quiz questions and constant cups of tea and my mum and dad, Deborah and John, sister and brother, Belle and Sebastian, and their partners, Harry and Colleen, and for their unwavering support and hilarious Zoom calls.

Finally, to Giles, my podcast partner, for just being the nicest and most supportive person out there. Thank you for dealing with me submitting bits for the book very late, messing up podcast audio, and my internet dropping out many, many times – always with kindness and compassion and grace – and for just being an absolutely brilliant person.

BLANK

GILES

First and foremost, a huge thank you to every single guest who has appeared on the *Blank Podcast*. Jim and I call it our weekly therapy session, and the podcast really has become that – a chance to sit and have these insightful and often profound conversations with such incredible people is truly a gift.

To Céline Hughes, for believing in this project and allowing us the freedom to express and channel our ideas, and to our copy-editor Gemma Wain for helping us to really craft this text.

Thank you to Baca's Coffee Bar in Seaford, where I wrote the bulk of my sections of the book. It's such a hub of kindness and wonderful coffee – thanks Nimeir, Sarah, Nikki, Ashley and Chloe.

To my amazing agent Becky, for always having my back, the team at Acast, Sam, Lizzy, and John, for supporting the show and being the best podcast host around, and the amazing Adam Buxton, for all the advice before we started.

A big thank you to Jon Ronson for his kind words of advice on writing non-fiction – they meant so much more than you realise – and Fiona Murden for her assistance in giving us a psychological point of view on blankness.

Thanks also to the amazing Paul Pilot for our amazing podcast theme music, to Nordic Bar for hosting us and our guests so many times, and Frequency café for the great room and special mocha coffees.

Thank you to podcastmerch.co.uk for all the wonderful T-shirts, mugs and tote bags.

To my wife, Michelle, and sons, Eli and Sonny, for always being patient and letting me waffle on through the process of writing this book.

Massive thanks to our wonderful listeners – your ongoing support and messages mean so much to us. And lastly, my comrade in this whole journey, Jim Daly – it's been so great working with you on this, and of course, the podcast itself. Your compassion and empathy go such a long way in what makes the show so successful. Love you, dude.